The Oldest Student at the Sorbonne

The Oldest Student at the Sorbonne

Russell Hodge

Published by Russell Hodge
PO Box 5555 Cronulla NSW 2230
russellhodgeauthor.com

First published 2018

© 2018 Russell Hodge

The moral right of the author has been asserted.

All rights reserved. Without limiting the rights under copyright restricted above, no part of this publication may be reproduced, stored in or introduced into a retrieval system, or transmitted, in any form or by any means (electronic, mechanical, photocopying, recording or otherwise), without the prior written permission of the copyright owner and publisher of this book.

A catalogue record for this book is available from the National Library of Australia

ISBN 978 0 6484489 0 7 (pbk)
     978 0 6484489 1 4 (ebk)

Designed and typeset by Blue Wren Books
bluewrenbooks.com.au

Cover images by Shutterstock and iStock

To Josie
Only she knows what life with me was like.

Author's note

I started writing this book while I was studying at the Sorbonne. Over the next six years, I began to make sense of what drove and motivated me to do things. All the events recounted actually occurred, and where possible, I have verified the events. Every event is my best recollection of what occurred and is told from my perspective. Every person referred to in the book existed although on occasions I have not used actual names. There are no composite personalities; the people described existed and lived as I, in hindsight, have perceived.

Prologue

I had slept rough before. The streets were my choice when in distress. Human beings when faced with danger or conflict choose flight or fight. I do flight. When I lost connection with people and reality, all I knew was that I had to escape.

I had a rule that while I slept on the street, I didn't look as if I slept on the street. I only took what was necessary; spare underpants, socks, shirts, razor blade and asthma medication in a small overnight bag. I emptied my pockets, and ensured that I had absolutely no identification. I didn't carry my driver's licence, jet-ski licence, seniors card, debit card, Medibank card, HCF card, library cards or RSL membership card.

I had slept on the streets of Sydney before but this time was different. I was going to Brisbane where no one knew me. Friends and family had become familiar with my sojourns and knew roughly where to look for me. I needed a change and as I was particularly distressed, I saw this move to Brisbane as being permanent.

I walked to the local station and waited for the train. I had no money so I didn't purchase a ticket. At Sutherland, I changed trains and caught the South Coast country train to Central. As I approached the ticket barrier a ticket inspector demanded, in broken English, to see my ticket. It was an absolute prerequisite in the NSW rail system that any person dealing with the public, particularly those who made announcements over the public address system didn't speak any version of English that was comprehensible. These attempts to communicate were very valuable. As passengers, strangers asked each other what was said and a sense of camaraderie was established. The good-natured bemusement created a bonhomie that raised the level of happiness of the commuters.

I looked the ticket collector straight in the eye and said, "je n'ai pas de billet" and walked straight past.

I scanned the departure board for my train to Brisbane. To my chagrin the next train to Brisbane was the following day. I had to apply my mind to the night's sleeping arrangements. I'd slept in a number of places. The immediately obvious place was the subway on Central Station adjacent to Platform 25. It was safe and other people stayed there but I didn't like it. It was a relatively narrow space and during the morning and afternoon peak hours it was packed with people. I sometimes sat on my mattress and watched the peak-hour crowds pass by. Each person in their own world rushing here, rushing there, some with music blasting in their ears, isolating them from their surrounds. I sat on the ground, a speck of flotsam and jetsam in a sea of humanity. Tossed from here to there, nudged, walked over, looked at with contempt and, very occasionally, smiled at.

I decided to sleep on Cathedral Street. The place of choice of many homeless, including me, was the square, adjacent to Cathedral Street opposite the Mathew Talbot hostel. The square was not really a square, but an irregularly shaped recreational area. It was bounded by Cathedral Street on one side and on the opposite side stood a dilapidated two-storey building at the end of which was the Woolloomooloo grocery store. A delicatessen, it also sold groceries and alcohol. To the left was the local chemist and police station. While the area was rundown it was still attractive. The buildings were angularly aligned, and there were tall trees and garden beds containing shrubs. The dominant feature, however, was the mammoth overhead structure that looked like the underside of a Roman aqueduct, but was in fact the Cahill Expressway. The juxtaposition of the buildings and the Cahill Expressway against the trees and shrubs constituted an eclectic beauty.

The homeless community had their own set of rules and behaviours. Each person had his or her own place in the square. Once you slept in a particular place it effectively became your space. The homeless community accepted every person who lived on the street. No one cared where you came from, how much money you had, what your status was, or why you were there. Acceptance was immediate and unconditional. No matter if you were a drug addict, mentally ill, ex-criminal, rich, poor, educated or uneducated—no one asked and no one cared, and newcomers were given all the assistance they needed.

When I first slept rough I needed to know where to eat, how to get mattresses and blankets, how to get clothes washed, where to store my meagre belongings, even find out what the time was. The homeless were swept off the street in the early morning and discouraged from returning until late afternoon. Skip bins in an adjacent enclosure were unlocked in the morning, locked during the day and unlocked late in the afternoon. Homeless people stored their belongings, usually blankets and mattresses, in these bins that were secured by a chain and padlock. Members of the homeless community held the keys. It ensured that their belongings were safe and secure.

I saw BK when I arrived. As I sat beside him I smiled as I recognised him as a friend although I was wary of him. I had known BK for a year; he was the first person who showed me where to sleep. Most people who slept rough were transients in difficult or disastrous situations, but BK slept rough by choice. Very few people choose this kind of life; it's a tough existence. People on the streets either have no other alternatives or suffer mental or addiction issues. BK had lived on the street for well over a decade and it showed. He was probably mid-fifties with straggly orange receding hair and an unkempt goatee beard. He was the archetypal homeless man insofar as sartorial elegance and personal hygiene were not high on his priorities. The average person would look askance at using these clothes to polish their car. He had filthy fingernails, grime around his neck, and teeth (what was left of them) that were yellow and discoloured. BK was an avid reader. He had a wide general knowledge, was keenly interested in politics, nationally and internationally, and was a student of the social issues of the day. He had a criminal record and had been severely bashed in the back of a police van in Darwin. He was great company and had an intimate knowledge of life on the street and how to survive.

But he could also be dangerous. On one occasion we were sitting, having a mild disagreement about the appropriateness of the chemist's sandwich board being on the footpath. Suddenly, he stood up, and lifted the sandwich board high over his head. I saw his eyes wide open and wild, his jaw fixed and menacing. He smashed me twice over the head with the sandwich board before I could escape. I was taken to hospital with severe concussion and neck and shoulder injuries, and my family had to be contacted to come and collect me. This taught me how to survive and be safe on the streets. I lived on the street as a shadow. While a shadow was present and real, it engaged with no one, left no imprint or mark on its surroundings and created no conflict or offence. Nobody assaulted a shadow. Understanding body language and facial expressions was an essential part of my tool-kit for surviving on the street. The school of hard knocks taught me when and how far to engage and how and when to retreat from my homeless friends.

It was now dark, although streetlights made it easy to see who was coming and going. I put my overnight bag on my chosen place of accommodation and searched for my mattress. I walked up Cathedral Street and pulled strips of cardboard out of garbage bins. I soon had enough cardboard to make a comfortable mattress. Cardboard was an excellent insulator from the cold emanating from the brick pavement. I sat on the mattress and contemplated how I could access the information I needed to be able to sleep, eat and wash in Brisbane the next day. I was calm, relaxed and felt safe. I had no one hassling or pressuring me, I had no responsibilities and I was accountable to no one.

Having established my place of lodging for the night, underneath the awning at the back of the chemist's shop, I settled in to watch people entering and leaving the grocery store across the square. Most people bought alcohol and cigarettes, a few bought groceries. They were a mix of old, young, male and female; a melting pot of the local community.

Two young women walked past me towards the store. They were very beautiful, although at my age any female younger than thirty looks beautiful.

I suddenly realised I was cold. I knew the Salvation Army provided blankets so I asked BK, who was dossing down with me that night, if the Salvos were coming.

"No, you'll have to give them a ring," he said. Not easy when you don't have a mobile phone.

I spotted Miss Universe and Miss World leaving the store, deep in conversation, ambling towards me. I called out, "Excuse me, girls."

Miss Universe looked across with disdain and quickened her pace. Miss World looked at me curiously.

"I don't want money," I told her.

Miss World grabbed her friend's arm and they walked towards me. I told them that I had just arrived, I was sleeping on the footpath tonight, that I was cold, and I needed blankets. I told them that the Salvos would provide blankets, and would they mind giving the Salvos a ring, and ask them to come to help me?

The girls said they would make the call and sauntered away. The conversation was short and their attitude dismissive and offhand. I felt they agreed to my request to shut me up, rather than any willingness to actually intercede with the Salvos on my behalf. I told myself I would give it half an hour, and if the Salvos hadn't come by then, I would try again.

About fifteen minutes later the girls returned. The disdainful girl asked me to move off my cardboard mattress so she could put a blanket on it. I dutifully obeyed and the other girl asked me to lie down so she could cover me with other blankets. I was taken aback by the request, but sensed a warmth and kindness that was hitherto absent. I instinctively obeyed; after all I am trained to obey young women. I had daughters about the same age and when they asked me to jump I always responded "how high?"

I saw that the blankets were woollen and brightly coloured. I was familiar with the Salvos blankets, which were thin, brown cotton, and, while welcome, not very warm.

"Where do these come from? They're not Salvos blankets."

"We got them from our beds," one of the girls said.

I was stunned by this gratuitous kindness to a complete stranger. I thought for a minute and said, "I am going to Brisbane tomorrow, where can I return them?"

She replied, "We don't want them back, can you give them to someone else?"

I told her about the bin where all our personal property was kept. "I'll put them in the bin tomorrow and someone who really needs them will welcome them," I said.

The girls put the blankets on me, tucked me in, and said goodnight. Their faces glowed with compassion and care. I went to sleep with a peaceful and calm heart. I slept soundly all night.

The next morning, I carefully folded the blankets and placed them in the homeless bin. I put all the cardboard back in the street bins. I left no trace of my existence.

One

There was no doubt—my studies at the Sorbonne University directly contributed to me living as an old homeless man, albeit temporarily, on the streets of Sydney. The question was, what had led me to enrol in the university at 66 years of age, with no real ability to speak French? This kind of decision-making was nothing new. Many years earlier I left my career as a schoolteacher, returned to university and became a solicitor, then left private practice as a solicitor to work full time in an aviation company, then later retired as a director of a public company before enrolling at the Sorbonne.

It was the eighteen-year chapter working for an aviation company that built my pathway to becoming a member of Sydney's most disadvantaged community. In 1994, after twenty years of practising as a solicitor, I became a director, and later a shareholder, of Pel-Air Aviation, a general aviation company that operated freight and medical evacuation flights. As the repository of legal knowledge within Pel-Air, I helped negotiate commercial deals and submit tenders.

For a while, the work was varied, interesting and pretty easy. Each day I had lunch with John Johnson, founder of Pel-Air, and other directors and shareholders. The aviation industry was difficult, but while most general aviation companies collapsed, Pel-Air survived and prospered.

However, by the late 1990s work at Pel-Air had become stressful and I worried that I wasn't doing a good job. I developed a habit of running regularly—by running I mean a perfect imitation of Forrest Gump. Nonetheless I ran about twelve kilometres most days. Over a three-month period I started to sleep less and run more, which increased my anxiety, so I slept even less and ran even longer, sometimes at three in the morning.

In 1996, my close friend Greg and I started a game of tennis. I served first. I threw the ball into the air and missed it.

"This is going to be easy," Greg called out.

"Get ready for the ace," I replied.

I threw the ball into the air and missed it by an even wider margin.

"You've got a head injury, I'm taking you home." As a former elite footballer, Greg was very familiar with head injuries, and he was concerned about my behaviour.

After extensive tests, I was diagnosed with severe depression, and was not able to work for more than three months. My recovery was slow. Initially I slept nearly eighteen hours a day, and I was so sick that I was unable to carry a cup of coffee without spilling it. I was only able to sit and watch the world go by.

Greg was the first person to understand my mental health difficulties, and certainly the first person outside my family to show empathy towards me in relation to my illness. No one else really understood what I was going through, with the exception of Josie, my wife. I 'recovered' and returned to normal without realising until too late that the words *normal* and *Russell* together made an oxymoron.

A few years after my collapse, Pel-Air won the Department of Defence contract to provide jets to train the Australian Navy and Air Force. For one month, I stayed in Baltimore in the United States, with John, where we lived while we purchased four Learjets that then had to be modified there, in order to carry out the tasks required under the contract.

On our return, I had overall responsibility for this part of the business. We employed fifteen alpha male former Australian Air Force fighter jet pilots, the Operations Manager reported to me, and each month I toddled into Maritime Headquarters on Garden Island to meet Jim, a squadron leader from the RAAF and the Contract Manager, to review our performance under the contract.

I liked the job, and got on very well with Jim, who would often ring Pel-Air and ask to speak to the 'Oxygen Bandit'. No matter who answered the phone, the call was always put through to me. Jim hated lawyers and schoolteachers, and thought their only value was in being canaries in a mine to test for poisonous gases.

We had seven jet aircraft based at HMAS Albatross, near Nowra, on the New South Wales south coast, where the Australian armed forces trained. We trained the ships to defend themselves against an enemy air attack. We had dogfights with Royal Australian Air Force F/A18 Hornet fighter jets and towed targets for these jets to shoot at. The Learjets towed targets that naval ships shot at for gunnery practice. They also flew one hundred and fifty feet above the water towards ships, simulating missile attacks that required radar operators to identify and lock onto the incoming aircraft. Sometimes mass simulated attacks on ships were planned in which Pel-Air participated with the Air Force.

One morning the Operations Manager arrived unannounced at my office in Mascot. The Ops Manager was an ex-fighter jet pilot who also flew jets under the contract. Roger was in his sixties, very bald, tall, straight-backed, slightly deaf with a loud voice, and would never be mistaken for a shrinking violet.

"I don't want to be Ops Manager any more, I just want to fly aircraft," he said.

"That's fine, Roger, when do you want to stop being Ops Manager?"

"In two weeks. And we have decided that John Roberts will be my replacement."

"I don't have a problem with that, I'm sure John will do a good job."

"Good, and his salary will be $200,000 a year," he said. This was a ninety percent increase in the current Ops Manager's salary.

"We're not going to pay that," I snapped.

"We've all got together and unanimously agreed on these terms. If you don't agree you won't have an Ops Manager," Roger declared, as he further straightened his back, and unblinkingly stared into my eyes. By 'we' I knew Roger meant all the pilots. The pilots were militant, and had two designated representatives to air their grievances, although Roger wasn't one of them. I understood now why Roger never contemplated a career as a diplomat.

The Ops Manager's job involved receiving a monthly program from the RAAF and Navy, broken down into a weekly, then daily program. The programs were in a form and language impossible for a layman to understand. Roger had me over a barrel, and he knew it. Without an Ops Manager, the business couldn't operate. Two weeks was not long enough to advertise and employ someone else. The mandatory requirement that the Ops Manager have a Secret Security Clearance made finding a replacement virtually impossible. I hated being bullied, stood over or dictated to. I was conflicted between the commercial imperative to maintain our contract, and my natural instinct to tell Roger to go fuck himself.

I had a couple of obvious choices: accede to the demand or negotiate. The directors agreed that these pilots were not about to compromise when they held all the cards. But there's always a way. My fellow directors, and owners of Pel-Air, were prepared to take the risk.

The next day I met Roger. I sat in front of him, and couldn't help but notice his self-satisfied smirk as he prepared to hear my capitulation.

"I've appointed a new Ops Manager. He starts in two weeks," I said.

"Who is it?" Roger couldn't hide his surprise and concern.

"You're looking at him. I start in two weeks, and you're going to give me all the training I need to do the job." The look on Roger's face was priceless.

"You can't do it, you don't have a security clearance."

"How do you think I get into MHQ each month, climb under the fence? Of course I've got a security clearance." We looked at each in silence, the air tense. I continued. "You're going to train me for the job, and we start right now. Show me how to read the program." I was not in the mood for discussion or argument.

After a week of confusing and inept instructions, Roger brought his resignation forward a week, and left me to it.

I approached Air Affairs, a company I knew, based next door, and asked them to show me how to read Pel-Air's program. Luckily, they were happy to help me after Roger's woefully inadequate training. With Air Affairs' help, I was able to retrieve the program each morning, and at least appear to do something.

I had been doing the job for about a week, muddling along, when I was approached by one of the younger pilots.

"You know you don't know what you're doing, Russell," Tim said.

"Yes, I know."

"You're going to fuck up the job, and lose the contract."

"That's right Tim, so you and your mates had better start looking for a job, cause it ain't gonna change."

We employed fifteen pilots, mostly self-funded retirees in their late fifties and sixties, and half a dozen young New Zealanders in their thirties with families to support. The difference between these two groups was encapsulated in a sign on the wall: "I would rather be an old fart, than a young dickhead."

Within twenty-four hours I had young pilots, with families to provide for, sitting on my shoulder helping me do the job. I worked at HMAS Albatross where the aircraft were based four days a week. I stayed three nights a week in bed and breakfasts near Berry, about half an hour drive from the base. I carried the program on my laptop so I was able to do the job remotely for the other three days. I really enjoyed being Ops Manager even though it meant being on call seven days a week.

Each Thursday night I had dinner with friends at the Blue Parrot in Cronulla. Invariably the phone rang during dinner, with a call from a ship's captain wanting to amend the program. Jo Gibson, the waitress, a very witty woman, would say in a loud voice, "Hold the phone, everyone, it's the Prime Minister calling—we have a national emergency." Jo never let me off the hook when I took a phone call during dinner.

Jo made a point. I determined that it was unacceptable that a ship's captain be able to call without notice to change the program. I changed things. With Commonwealth approval, changes to the program required at least forty-eight hours' notice, except where a critically important training exercise was involved. It made my life easier.

After nine months, the pilot body approached me again, and suggested I retire back to Sydney. At the same time my fellow directors wanted me back in Sydney. John Roberts, the pilots' previously recommended Operations Manager, took over my job, at an increased but reasonable salary. The pilots were ecstatic, Jim and the Commonwealth were over the moon, and the Pel-Air directors were relieved we still had the contract. Everyone was happy—well, almost everyone.

It wasn't long before a casual lunchtime conversation changed our lives.

"I was with Bridgey yesterday and he told me some Singaporeans wanted to buy his airline. They wanted him to give it away, so he told them to get lost." This was Keith, our Managing Director. Bridgey was one of the owners of Air North, an airline based in Darwin.

"Who are the Singaporeans?" I asked.

"The guys who bought Hazelton and Kendall when they went broke," Keith said.

"Why don't they buy us?" I asked. Pel-Air was a very profitable, well-managed business which made it a very saleable company.

I was soon in touch with Kim Hai, the executive chairman of REX. We agreed on a price based on earnings supported by assets. Kim Hai needed to float REX on the Sydney Stock Exchange to raise money to pay for the Pel-Air shares. Kim Hai had a meticulous attention to detail and the negotiations were very protracted. We were able to complete the sale contract subject to the float being successful.

After contracts were signed and the prospectus issued, I became part of the roadshow through regional New South Wales to persuade people to subscribe to the upcoming float. The roadshow was headed by John Sharpe, an ex-Commonwealth Transport Minister. At each stop the same presentation was made. To amuse ourselves we played a game; I gave John a word he was required to seamlessly use in his presentation to potential investors. John introduced 'mortification', 'reptilian' and 'peripatetic' into his repertoire. He was never beaten. The roadshow was fun and a great success. After REX was floated on the Sydney Stock Exchange I was appointed to the board, and subsequently became Chairman of its Safety and Risk Committee.

I worked full time for REX, and was an executive director responsible for Pel-Air. Working for a public company was challenging. I was used to freedom, making decisions with little consultation, and pretty well doing what I liked. Kim Hai made everyone, particularly me, accountable. I had to ensure Pel-Air met the profit targets we had guaranteed for the next three years.

Everything I did, every decision I wanted to make, had to be approved by Kim Hai. On many occasions we clashed, and in one year, I resigned three times. Despite the culture shock, being a director of a successful airline was very rewarding. Kim Hai was very demanding, and never suffered fools gladly (except perhaps me). When he first took control of the airline it was a financial basket case; despite not having any previous experience in the aviation industry, he reversed the airline's financial state by implementing a business model unique to the industry. His greater achievement was the sense of family and pride he engendered in the workplace.

On the 18th November 2009 Josie and I drove to Dubbo to deal with some REX issues. I had decided to combine business with pleasure. We booked into a local motel and enjoyed a convivial dinner in a local restaurant. I was busy with REX and Pel-Air and Josie had a busy life helping our children, and looking after grandchildren. It was a welcome relief for us to travel together away from Sydney.

It was about ten p.m., and we had just settled back into our room when my mobile rang. It was Jim Davis, Managing Director of REX. "I've some bad news. NGA is missing on a flight to Norfolk Island." By NGA I knew he meant one of our Westwind jets. The news hit me like a bolt from the blue. Josie saw the look on my face.

"What's wrong?" she said.

"One of our aircraft is missing. We have to go back to Sydney."

Josie suggested she drive, a good suggestion. She had better eyesight, better reflexes, controlled the car better, and drove the car more quickly and safely than me.

I rang Jim in the car. He told me that one of our Westwinds, VH-NGA with two crew on board and four passengers was missing off the coast of Norfolk Island. The flight was a medical evacuation flight from Apia in Samoa to Sydney via Norfolk Island. There was no news except it had crashed into the ocean.

I was beside myself. I had asthma, and I had very bad coughing fits on the way back to Sydney. Despite Josie assuring me that I couldn't assume the worst, that miracles happened, and there was nothing I could do about it, my stress levels went through the roof. The prospect of people dying was too horrible for me to contemplate.

Two hours later my mobile rang.

"Everyone's safe," Jim said. "NGA ditched into the sea and

everyone on board got out. It appears no one was injured. When will you get here?"

"That's a huge relief," I said. "I'll be there in an hour."

I arrived at the boardroom at about three a.m., with all senior executives, chief pilot, and standards manager elated at the outcome.

Despite the fact that everyone survived, it would be treated as a fatal accident and the Civil Aviation Safety Authority would probably shut down all Pel-Air's operations—a commercial disaster. Before representatives from the CASA arrived, I made two decisions. The first was to ground the medical evacuation operation. The second was to make all information available to CASA.

When CASA arrived, I told them of my decisions. CASA provided me a long list of information and documentation it required. At the next meeting twenty-four hours later, I had piles of files and documents carefully matched to every CASA query. It made their task straightforward. I provided details of all pilots and management personnel so CASA had free, unfettered and unfiltered access to all staff. This was a critical decision, and for a lawyer very unusual. I gave CASA access to staff and reports that were well in excess of Pel-Air's legal obligations. After a short investigation, CASA allowed the Metroliners and the military contract aircraft to continue operating. Only a small part of the aircraft operation was affected.

It soon became clear that the aircraft, crewed by captain Dominic James and co-pilot Zoe Cupit, ran out of fuel due to bad weather at Norfolk Island, and had to ditch into the ocean. There were four passengers—a nurse, a doctor, the patient and the patient's husband. It was a dark night and there was a two-metre swell. If Dominic tried to land at Norfolk with nil visibility the aircraft would have run off the end of the runway over the cliffs and everyone would have perished. Dominic landed the aircraft blind in the ocean. After the impact, with the aircraft sinking, he left his seat, and opened the escape hatch. Zoe and the passengers, including the patient who had to be unstrapped from the stretcher, escaped into the ocean. All six persons, three of whom were wearing lifejackets, clung to each other. The night was dark and they were more than a kilometre from a desolate coast.

Dominic had a torch in his pocket. Crew always carried torches, but rarely in their pockets. Dominic shone the torch and someone from the airport rescue service saw the dim light in the distance. This person alerted the authorities, and a rescue boat arrived. It was a miracle.

The reason for the crash was obvious. Despite the flight being three and a half hours, Dominic had failed to completely fill the fuel tanks. In one hundred and eighty-five previous planned flights of three and a half to four hours to a remote aerodrome at night, every Pel-Air captain carried full fuel. On the same flight seven weeks earlier, Dominic completely filled the fuel tanks. I was in the room when he was asked immediately after the accident why he didn't fill up the tanks.

"I don't know," he said. You could have heard a one-hundred-dollar note fall on the carpet. The air was thick with disbelief.

The impact on the occupants of the aircraft was severe, and the nurse, doctor and patient never recovered from their injuries. The inevitable investigation took its toll. CASA audited Pel-Air and produced a report that contained requests for corrective action.

A *60 Minutes* report in March 2010 blamed Dominic for the accident but the tide soon turned and I became increasingly anxious as the blame started to shift to Pel-Air. I took this personally. I accepted criticism that demonstrated

Pel-Air was deficient in some areas. These deficiencies were all quickly rectified but the issue remained: to what extent did these deficiencies cause or contribute to the accident. I had difficulty sleeping. I was often sick in the stomach, and my asthma attacks became more frequent and severe. The stress, as usual, impacted on my relationships with those close to me. I carried the guilt that I could have some responsibility for the permanent injury to the passengers and the huge commercial losses Pel-Air sustained.

I started to feel that I could have abrogated my legal and moral responsibilities with respect to Pel-Air's operations. I had always thought that mere legal compliance was never sufficient. Years earlier I had instituted a fatigue management system into Pel-Air when it wasn't a legal requirement to do so because I believed it was the right thing to do. Pel-Air was the second aviation company in Australia to implement a CASA-approved Fatigue Management System.

After REX bought all Pel-Air shares, as well as being appointed to the REX board, I remained on the Pel-Air board of directors. I never applied my mind to what that really meant, and what heavy responsibilities I had shouldered. I knew Section 28 of the Civil Aviation Act required directors to take reasonable steps to ensure every activity of Pel-Air was done with reasonable care and diligence. Being a director I was liable if there was inadequate management control or supervision of employees.

Dominic and Zoe's account of the refuelling of the aircraft greatly disturbed me. In separate interviews, they each provided the same account of the refuelling procedure. Dominic refuelled the aircraft, and as they sat in the cockpit with the fuel tanker parked alongside, Zoe told Dominic the aircraft wasn't full of fuel and asked him if they should refuel to capacity. Dominic said he had enough fuel to get to Norfolk

Island. He deliberately chose to take off with the fuel tanks eighty-three percent full. Why didn't he take the hint that Zoe gave him? Why had he totally filled the fuel tanks on the same flight seven weeks earlier, but not this time? Why, when he was flying thousands of kilometres to a speck in the ocean with changeable weather, wouldn't he take the simple step of opening two valves to fill the aircraft choc-a-block with fuel? After all, he did the external inspection of the aircraft, and he could have pulled the valves that opened the wing tip tanks as he walked past. Had he done so, there wouldn't have been an accident. Legally he didn't have to fill the tanks but why didn't he? The lack of an explanation was frustrating. Pel-Air's Operations Manual, approved by CASA, set out the minimum fuel required to be carried on all flights. Pel-Air's culture on these particular types of flights was absolutely clear: ignore the Operations Manual and fill the aircraft to the brim with fuel. Dominic refuelled in accordance with the legal minimum requirements, as he was entitled to do. He ignored Pel-Air's culture, as he was entitled to do. In all previous one hundred and eighty-five flights of this nature, every captain, including Dominic, filled the aircraft. We failed to enshrine the culture into Pel-Air's Operations Manual. If we had done so Dominic wouldn't have had a choice; he would have had to carry as much fuel as possible. That's where my guilt lay.

The shock waves from the accident never stopped. I carried my burden of guilt to the Sorbonne and beyond. Still, life moved on; myself to retirement, Dominic to fly jets for another medical evacuation company, Zoe to fly for Virgin Airlines, and the patient committed suicide.

Eighteen months after the accident I organised a holiday with friends on the Canal du Midi in France. The day before Josie and I left for our holiday I was due to settle a sale of my shares in REX. The negotiations had been very protracted, mired in conflict, and made me sick in the stomach. I looked forward to the arrival of a substantial amount of money into my bank account, a nice start to the holiday.

On the day of settlement my solicitor told me the Australian Competition and Consumer Commission had blocked the sale. I was disappointed, but I had been around long enough to know a deal is never done until the money's in the bank.

My cares, stress and worries dissipated quickly on the Canal du Midi. After a week on the canal Josie and I had a week in Kassell in Holland where we met her mother, who was also on holidays. Josie's parents were Dutch migrants who came to Australia in 1950 with nothing.

Seeing where her mother grew up, where she met Josie's father, and riding our bikes with Josie's seventy-five-year-old aunt took me into a new world, an old interesting world, far away from REX. For once I only lived for each day, until I arrived at Heathrow Airport on the way home.

I sat in front of a computer at Heathrow Airport on the 14th of June 2011, and resigned as a director of REX. I'm not sure why, although perhaps after a stress-free holiday, I imagined there was another life. Maybe it was a spur-of-the-moment emotional decision, or that I subconsciously realised the impact on my health the Norfolk Island accident had had and I didn't want to take the chance of it happening again.

My retirement was sudden and yet, it wasn't. Before I even thought of retirement, I enrolled to study French part time at Sydney University.

Years before, a holiday in France in the Minervois, and attending the Paris Air show and negotiating aircraft contracts, had piqued my interest in French. I liked Paris and the French people.

After my resignation from REX I did more subjects, and during the semester, I heard about the student exchange scheme. I thought it would be interesting and challenging to study in Paris. I went to the information sessions, and quickly identified the Sorbonne as the best place to study.

As a young student at Sydney Teachers College, I'd had a weekly two-hour tutorial with Bill Collins, who later became a famous film critic. His tutorials in 'Foundations of Education', based on philosophy, were finished in what seemed like a heartbeat. His description of dialectic teaching stayed with me forever. I have practised it as a teaching method all my life. My teaching by questioning drove my children and grandchildren mental. They wanted to be given an answer, rather than having to work things out for themselves. It was only natural that I studied at the Sorbonne as I regarded it as the pinnacle of university education in philosophy.

My main concern was my age. I qualified for the application, having achieved a credit average in my French subjects. There was no ageism at the university. Dr. Sonia Wilson my French lecturer and the university international department encouraged me to apply for the exchange. Having been accepted for study at the Sorbonne, I simply had to go through the process of visas, enrolments, accommodation and travel plans.

It was typical of me. I decided to study at the Sorbonne, and didn't consider the consequences, or difficulties. Josie didn't want me to go. Some of my friends doubted that I would succeed, particularly those who spoke French. I never considered that my previous breakdown and depression, or my self-imposed pressure to succeed, could result in unusual, if not bizarre behaviour. I was hell-bent on going to the Sorbonne.

Two

I arrived at Gare de L'Est in Paris in late August 2012. Gare de L'Est was the equivalent of Central Railway Station in Sydney; they both teemed with people rushing purposively in every direction. Subterranean platforms serviced by long escalators led somewhere, yet nowhere. Crowds formed and disappeared like waves as trains arrived and left platforms.

I gradually became aware of a significant difference. Young men in uniform carried machine guns. Standing in pairs, they were ever watchful, their fingers on the trigger. I found this disconcerting, and I was a little apprehensive as to the hidden danger that apparently lurked beneath the everyday life of the Parisian commuter.

There were multiple exits with signage, unsurprisingly all in French. I had all the belongings I needed for a six-month stay in Paris—a laptop, and clothing jammed into a huge suitcase. I stood motionless and confused, trying to determine which exit to take. Inexplicably I decided to catch a train from Charles de Gaulle airport to my destination. I had just finished building a waterfront home in Sydney's Cronulla, so the cost of a taxi to my destination was inconsequential.

Perhaps I came to Paris with a student rather than a tourist mentality, or perhaps it was a subconscious portent of my future.

I had arranged a home stay, with a room in an apartment that overlooked the Canal Saint-Matin. The canal was described in tourist brochures as being very picturesque. The other attraction was that the owner of the apartment, my putative host, Damien, was supposedly used to hosting students. I assumed that this meant that the facilities were likely to be student friendly, and more importantly I would have an opportunity to practise speaking French. I had initially thought that a home stay with a family would be better. I had a wife, four children and grandchildren. At home, I had constant contact with my children and grandchildren, so I thought staying with a family would provide me with a familiar family environment. The family could help me improve my French and, in return, I could teach the children English. However, after emails back and forth with Damien in which it was obvious he frequently hosted international students, I came to the conclusion that staying with him was the better option.

I took a guess, and chose an exit that I thought would lead in the general direction of the Canal Saint-Matin. I stepped outside the station onto a very wide bitumen area about fifty metres wide that provided access for cars and buses. I typed the address on my mobile phone, looked at the directions on the screen and started the trudge to my future, if temporary, home. I was excited by the prospect of university study in Paris but tired after the long flight in economy class from Sydney. I headed for the corner of the bitumen and crossed a wide thoroughfare. On the corner was a restaurant and bar, typical in Paris. I started to walk down a road with a garden divide separating the traffic. I couldn't but help notice a homeless man sitting on the footpath with a bowl at his feet.

I lived in the southern suburbs of Sydney and didn't see a homeless person from one day to the next. I had never met a homeless person. He appeared to be in his early thirties. I noticed his boots were old with holes in the soles. He wore a faded overcoat, old brown trousers tied at the top with what appeared to be a rope. He was as unobtrusive as a garbage bin on the footpath. He sat against the wall of the restaurant and I gave him a wide berth, as I didn't want to engage with him. I was disturbed by a Paris I hadn't envisaged—guns and poverty. I guess, even at sixty-six, I was still naïve.

I walked down a flight of steps, veered to the right, and the famous Canal Saint-Matin came into view. Beauty and art exist in context. I looked at the canal and instead of art I saw a long bathtub filled with water that had just been occupied by a couple of ten-year-old boys rolling in the mud. It was very long and stretched into the distance in both directions. Swimming across it wouldn't constitute exercise. There were no boats, people or birds to soften or create interest. There was detritus floating on the surface of the water. I stood and looked and listened. Both sides of the canal were very similar. Next to the side of the canal where I stood was a concrete footpath, then a grass verge and a two-lane road bounded by rows of low-rise apartments. The canal was like a lung. It allowed the apartments to breathe; it created a sense of space, calm and yes, beauty.

I identified the apartment block where I was staying, and walked through a gate to the locked door on the ground floor. There was a pad with each apartment numbered and a button to push to speak to an occupant.

I pressed the button.

A male voice answered, "Bonjour."

"Bonjour, je m'appelle Russell."

The voice quickly said something in French that I didn't understand. I thought it was French even though the voice spoke so quickly I couldn't grasp a single syllable.

I said, "Repetez, s'il vous plait."

The voice replied with something totally unintelligible.

I repeated, "Repetez s'il vous plait."

The voice said, "First floor, first door on the left."

I knocked on the door and it opened and we exchanged greetings. A man introduced himself in English as Damien and I reintroduced myself in French.

Damien was a man of medium build and looked to be in his early fifties. He wore black-rimmed glasses, and was dressed in casual slacks and an un-ironed shirt. His short black hair was somewhat unkempt but his smile was warm and welcoming. He asked me to come in, and I asked, in French, that we talk only in French. Damien nodded his head, and spoke to me in French. I thought it was French. I asked him to repeat himself a couple of times. In fairness, he did as I asked, however, on each occasion he repeated what he said even more quickly. The result was that I was totally unable to communicate with him.

On about the third repetition he said in stilted English, "Welcome to your new home. I hope you have had a good trip. You must be tired—would you like a cup of coffee?"

I was quite upset by my initial encounter with Damien. The raison d'etre of my stay with Damien was to speak French on a daily basis. I had the impression that Damien was making no attempt to speak to me in French, and in fact by speaking very quickly, he was ensuring it would be impossible for me to communicate in my chosen language.

He opened the lounge room door and ushered me inside. I'd agreed to stay with Damien but I didn't realise another family also lived in the apartment; a mother and daughter.

They looked like large rats, with short dumpy legs and rat-like whiskers, but were in fact fox terriers. Mum was docile and obedient and was happy to sit on Dad's (Damien's) lap. The child was exuberant, disobedient and, like all children, jumped all over the lounge. Damien looked at his dogs, and spoke about them as if they were his children.

I glanced around the lounge room, and noticed an old red sofa with black stains on it. A red sheet was used to cover the stains but the child dog had ripped the sheet. An equally dilapidated chair of the same set faced an old television set parked in the corner of the room. In the other corner was a very tarnished table surrounded by four chairs. Damien told me that this was the dining table but it was only used when more than two people came to dinner. As he introduced me to his dogs, and talked about the table, any pretence or attempt to speak French had vanished. I looked around the room while reflecting on the furniture and the dogs. I knew that if this furniture were to be discarded on a council clean-up in Sydney no self-respecting scavenger would take it.

Paradoxically, Damien's reluctance to speak French and the state of the lounge room with its old furniture and feral dogs left me feeling calm and relaxed. About to study philosophy at the Sorbonne, I reflected on why I would leave a brand-new, waterfront home in Sydney with brand-new furniture, and yet be happy and comfortable in an unhygienic dump in Paris, surrounded by dogs.

I concluded that we are what we experience. Virtually all our reactions are based in some way on what we have experienced either directly or indirectly in the past. As a consequence, our personality, likes, dislikes, the way we behave is based on, or influenced by experience. The application of experience to subsequent events is from both emotional and intellectual perspectives. A good experience in one situation translates to a good experience in another, similar situation. Despite my frustration with our level of communication I was happy and relaxed as I sat in Damien's room as some of my happiest memories as a teenager related to living with big dogs in an even shabbier room.

My family settled in Hill End west of Bathurst in the 1850s. They were sheep farmers. In the 1850s there was gold mining and some reasonably fertile land, however my family chose to farm marginal land. Two of my grandfather's brothers ran a sheep farm about three to six miles, depending on which part of the farm you stood, from the Hill End township. The Hill End township was one pub and one general store.

One of the brothers was my Uncle Roly. While I was studying at Sydney University in my late teens, I spent time with Roly. Role, as I called him, was in his early sixties and lived at Maitland Camp. He never married and lived alone. He wore the same clothes every day; dirty brown boots, dark grey trousers, a flannelette shirt and a hat. He was short, walked with a stoop, had skin cancer sores on his balding head and had a disfigured lip caused by cancer from smoking. The part of him I noticed the most was his neck. It sat above the collar of his shirt and was crinkled with what appeared to be masses of large pimples and dirt ingrained in the grooves of his neck. I was the only person who was prepared to stay with him.

Maitland Camp was a weatherboard cottage much older than Role that had never been painted. It consisted of a lounge room, kitchen, and two bedrooms. There was an external shed with some tank water to wash and an outside toilet that he called a 'dunny'. There was no bath, no shower, no washing machine or dryer, no running water. The dunny was a pit surrounded by four walls of tin and a makeshift metal roof. When I went to the dunny, Role said I must always check for red bellied black snakes. The kitchen had a sink and a wood stove. I used to wash my hands and face in the kitchen sink. The cottage was set back about fifty metres from a dirt road that ran past the cottage and led to Hill End. Between the cottage and the road was a small apple and pear orchard. There was never any fruit—the birds always got there first. On the road side of the cottage was a veranda covered by a leaky iron roof, broken boards for a floor and a veranda rail with rotting timber. The entrance to the cottage led directly into the lounge room. The lounge room had a huge fireplace that I could stand up in. There was always a fire, summer and winter, and a kettle of boiling water always hung from a hook suspended across the fireplace. Role, like others in the Hodge family, was an alcoholic. After a very bad accident driving home drunk one night, he substituted alcohol with an endless consumption of tea. Dumped in the lounge room were a dresser, one sofa and two chairs. The 'furniture' was at least sixty years old and dilapidated beyond repair; any semblance of cover barely existed. The piece de resistance was the two dogs. Hill End farmers used Kelpies and Role's Kelpies lived on the lounge. They spent the whole day sleeping on the lounge. Role loved his dogs, as did I.

We spent hours on the balcony drinking tea. He told me stories of his days as a fourteen-year-old driving a team of bullocks pulling a dray laden with bales of wool to Bathurst. He told me about the conflicts between the Chinese and English gold miners. I learnt of the local characters, what they did and where they lived. Occasionally we went to the paddock to round up sheep. Our one argument was the issue of wearing shoes. I didn't wear shoes until I went to high school. Of course, at university I wore shoes, but never at Hill End. Role insisted I wore shoes and I refused. One day when we were in a paddock, to teach me a lesson, he deliberately walked me through a patch of hard-backed thistles. My feet were so hard I didn't notice. He never again demanded I wear shoes.

He told me about my grandfather, his eldest brother Russell, who I was named after as the first grandchild. My grandfather was famous. He was headmaster of Maitland Boys High School and, at the time, the most senior headmaster in the New South Wales Department of Education. He was listed in the Who's Who of Australians in 1956. He lived with my grandmother on the school grounds. My grandparents lived in a beautiful colonial mansion called Hinder House. I only stayed with my grandfather once when I was a boy however, I never saw my grandfather—he was too busy. My parents took myself and brothers and sisters to visit my grandparents after their retirement. My most vivid recollections are of being excluded from adult conversation, and being sent outside with a two-pronged trowel and bucket, with my brother Greg, to weed the lawn.

On one occasion, our family and friends of my parents visited my grandfather. As everyone was leaving, my dimwit Uncle Wal asked my grandfather why he called his house Halcyon. I was fourteen years old. My parents and friends stood transfixed while this brilliant educator discussed the origins of the word halcyon. Halcyon was a bird of Greek legend that made a floating nest in the Aegean sea, and had the power to calm the waves while waiting for the arrival of her chicks. Hence in my grandfather's house, where he settled after his retirement, peace and calm prevailed.

I often went rabbit shooting. The ritual was always the same. First I walked to the old dresser surviving on a wall of the lounge and picked up the single shot .22 rifle leaning against the wall. Role watched me like a hawk as I removed bullets from the drawer of the dresser, and put them in my pocket. I was absolutely forbidden to carry a loaded rifle while walking. Then I picked up the rifle and walked to the door. Finally I heard high-pitched cackling masquerading as a laugh.

"Going out to scare the rabbits, are you?"

"No," I defiantly retorted. "I am going out to bring home our dinner."

I never did.

Role showed me how to divine for water. Water was scarce in Hill End, and a lot of water came from bores that tapped into underground streams. The problem was finding where underground streams were located. Role showed me how to take a green forked stick, and hold it in my hands with my palms pointing up. I held the stick by the two prongs with the single part of the stick facing away from my body. It was impossible for the straight part of the stick to bend. I started at the side of the cottage and walked towards the road. As I neared the road the stick gradually pointed to the ground. The force became so strong I could no longer hold the stick so I knew there was an underground stream beneath my feet. I could divine for water. Not everyone could do it. It was not a skill. Some people can play music by ear, others cannot, some people can divine water, others cannot. It was the sole method of finding water in Hill End in the nineteenth and early twentieth centuries.

I also worked with Harry. Harry Whiteman, Role's brother-in-law, owned a sheep farm on the Macquarie River where the country was very steep. Farmers increased their usable acreage by felling trees. Harry's land was so steep it had to be cleared by hand. I spent months with Harry on steep countryside ringbarking trees with an axe, and digging out suckers with a mattock. Role suggested we make an axe and a mattock as a single tool. In an old shed near his house Role had a blacksmith forge. He took an old axle from a car and an old axe handle and heated the forge. He supervised me while I heated the axle in the forge, put it on the forge and used a forging hammer to mould the axle into the shape of a mattock on one end and an axe on the other. I expanded the iron and punched a hole in the middle where the axe handle would fit. I had loads of satisfaction swinging that tool I made with my bare hands.

My tour of Damien's apartment continued. I had a bedroom that doubled as a study space. It was well set up for students. The single bed was comfortable and the wardrobe space was adequate. There was a desk with drawers and, importantly, Internet connection.

I was excited about exploring Paris and starting my studies at the Sorbonne. I felt like a teenager on a first date.

Three

In the afternoon, I set out to explore the local area. To be settled and happy in Paris I needed to organise food, transport and my university enrolment, and of the three, the overwhelming priority was food. I needed to find a regular place to eat within walking distance of my new home—routine was the root of my emotional stability.

I discovered there were a dozen eating establishments within a short walking distance of my apartment. There were no cafés; the Parisian equivalent of the Sydney café was a restaurant/bar. Visually they were depressingly similar to each other. Usually at the bottom of a multi-storey building, they were identified with a red awning overhanging small groups of tables and chairs on the footpath. Signage on the awnings such as Café de l'Est, Schmidt 1904, Fruit de Mer, Les Tramway, identified the restaurant.

I walked down a street close to home, past a commercial establishment that had a blue awning. At first I didn't identify it as a restaurant/bar. The footpath was extremely narrow and there was room for only three tables. The sign on the footpath—"VENDREDI 19EU POT AU FEU maison"—

protruded onto the adjacent rue. The establishment was narrow and the entrance made even narrower by the fact it was a single door. The rest of the small frontage was timber, covered with signs advertising community activities. I walked inside. The place had about twelve tables surrounded by chairs and was dingy. There was a small bar with the usual array of liquor displayed and a row of bar stools for customers at the edge of the bar.

Damien had warned me of the arrogance of French barmen. "They will be very impatient with you and will not like the way you try to speak French," he said. "You will also find they are very rude."

I asked him why they were like that and he said, "They just are."

So it was with some trepidation I approached the bar. The barman was a very thin man with somewhat tousled hair. In keeping with the bar, he appeared a bit dishevelled.

I discovered that he spoke no English at all. I ordered a black coffee and sat at the bar. Coffee cost €1 if I sat at the bar and €2 if I sat at a table, which was common in Paris. I ordered a second coffee and left.

I made a repeat visit the next day. I entered the bar, ordered one black coffee, then another and left. The third day, I again entered the bar and sat down. Once was unique, twice was coincidence, three times was habit. The barman gave me a welcoming smile and extended his hand and I shook it. I didn't know whether he was congratulating me on my repeated visits or giving me a genuine welcome.

He said, "Je m'appelle Farid."

"Je m'appelle Russell."

We had a stilted conversation. I was able to explain that I was a student at the Sorbonne studying philosophy, and that I lived nearby beside the canal. I didn't want to eat there but at least I had found a pleasant place where I could relax and feel comfortable.

The next afternoon, having spent the day riding a bike, I was exhausted. I was too tired to try a restaurant so I decided to wander down to Farid's for a meal. Farid welcomed me with a handshake.

I said, "Manger, s'il vous plait."

I asked for the menu, and he handed it to me. The menu was a piece of cardboard with a single entry—couscous. I had heard of couscous but had no idea what it was. Nonetheless I requested it.

A short time later black coffee and freshly squeezed orange juice arrived at my table. A middle-aged man wearing an apron appeared and placed the couscous in front of me. It came in four parts; an empty bowl, a plate with a substance that resembled finely chopped cheese, a bowl of vegetable soup and a plate of meat consisting of beef, sausage and chicken. I stared at the plates wondering what to do. The most obvious was to pick up the bowl, drink the soup, cut up and eat the meat, then tip the yellowish substance, which looked inedible, into the garbage bin. Except I was really hungry.

I asked the man who delivered the meal, whom I assumed was the cook, how to eat it. He put the yellow substance in the empty bowl, added vegetables from the soup bowl on top, then ladled some soup into the bowl, and finally cut the meat which he placed round the edge of the bowl. I ate it quickly and greedily. The meal was delicious.

As I left I give Farid a €50 note and he gave me €35 change. He knew my French was limited so he not only gave me a receipt but carefully counted the change identifying each note and coin so that I knew exactly what the meal cost and how the change was calculated.

***

I was senior partner of Owen Hodge & Son solicitors in Sydney. My father, Owen founded the legal practice in 1951. He served in the armed forces in World War II and married my mother in England near the end of the war. On his return to Australia, he recommenced his law school studies, and was still at Sydney University law school when I and my brother and sister were born. He graduated with second-class honours in law, and established his own practice. I joined the practice in 1971 after I graduated with a Bachelor of Laws from the Australian National University.

My father was a sole practitioner who had no ambition to grow the practice. He was averse to risk. I was and am a risk taker. During the twenty-year period in which I was a partner the practice grew significantly, however circumstances led to me leaving the firm, to establish a practice in the bedroom of a rented house.

In 1993, after 20 years working as a partner in Owen Hodge & Son, it was important that I separated work from home. So every morning I got up, showered, put on a suit and drove my children to primary school en route to the coffee shop. In this way I left home for work. After breakfast at the coffee shop, I returned home to my 'office'. At the end of the day, I left the 'office' (shut the bedroom door), changed into casual clothes, forgot about work, and would then be home. My home legal practice, specialising in aviation law, was very successful. For the seven years I practised at home, I never lost the habit of starting the day with breakfast at the local café.

For the previous twelve months, I had frequented Mim's on Woolooware Road. I went to Mim's rain, hail, or shine seven days a week, and it was always the same—three-egg omelette but only one egg yolk, spinach, roast tomato and a large weak soy cappuccino. Unlike the streets of Paris where the footpaths were generally narrow, the footpath outside Mim's was quite wide, and there were many tables on the footpath. The café was not so large as to lose a sense of intimacy and yet not so small that I felt I was eating alone. The café catered for tradespersons in the early morning and an assortment of people during the morning, lunch and early afternoon. It was a local meeting place, ideal for socialising. Mim's was bright, open and tastefully decorated. The nature of the interior reflected the customers; a degree of wealth and sophistication but not in an overtly ostentatious manner. Mim, the owner, was a single mum, about forty years old, slim and attractive with short curly brown hair and blessed with a friendly and engaging personality.

Each morning, while eating breakfast and reading *The Sydney Morning Herald* at Mim's, I was not to know that my journey to study philosophy had already begun. Aristotle and Descartes would have enjoyed breakfast with me at Mim's. Aristotle thought that the mind and body acted together, Descartes thought the body and mind were totally separate. Mim's given name was Dominique. This was shortened to both Mim and Dom. Not Yin and Yang, but Mim and Dom. Each nomenclature had its separate domain. I was in the Mim domain.

The café's customers, strangers and passersby, occupied the Mim domain and called her Mim. In this domain Mim was always cheerful, pleasant and obliging. Staff, family, friends, suppliers and persons close to her occupied the Dom domain and called her Dom. I sometimes wondered what it would be like to inhabit the Dom domain. I suspected that this domain would reveal significantly wider ranges of emotions, feelings and character flaws than existed in the Mim domain. If I was in the Dom domain, would I like Dom or would she like me? Even more importantly, was it possible to live simultaneously in both domains? If Aristotle and Descartes were not dead, we would be at an outside table, an umbrella shielding us from the hot summer sun, discussing if either Mim or Dom acted independently of her body.

I visited Farid most days. Sometimes just for coffee, sometimes for a meal. He always shook my hand and introduced me to other customers. He explained to them who I was and that I needed help with the language. Farid was one of the many Algerian migrants in Paris. Farid's bar became one of the rocks on which my stay in Paris would be based.

I walked down Boulevarde St. Michel. My holiday couldn't continue indefinitely and it was time to enrol. After all, the reason I was in Paris was to study philosophy. The Sorbonne was everything I expected. Security guards stood at the door of a very old sandstone building. I approached the entrance when a security guard called out in French.

"Stop! You cannot enter!"

"Why not?" I said.

"Only students are allowed to enter."

"I am a student."

"No, you are not," he laughed.

I produced a letter from Sorbonne University advising that I had been accepted into the Sorbonne as a philosophy student.

I heard the guard say some words, "inscrire (enrol), internationale (international), etudiant (student) and E." I surmised that the enrolment office for international students was in corridor E. There were other words he said such as "proche", "escalier", "entrée", that I assumed meant the enrolment office was upstairs near the entrance. Perceptions and first impressions can be misleading. I suspected the security guard regarded me as a curious old man not entitled to enter the university.

I walked through the corridors looking for corridor E. I was enthralled. It was a beautiful old sandstone university with wide corridors and extremely high ceilings. It was like walking back in history. I found corridor E and searched every room. There was no enrolment office. Two young people walked toward me.

"Parlez vous Anglais?" In unison, they said "Non." An older person approached. The conversation was identical. After the fourth attempt, I realised English was a forbidden language in this elite Paris university.

I decided to start again and walk back to the entrance. I had now traversed every corridor, on multiple floors, in this part of the Sorbonne. As I approached the entrance, I noticed a sign with the letter 'I' attached to the wall at the start of a corridor. The penny dropped. The letter 'I' in French is pronounced 'E'. I walked towards the corridor, up the stairs and into the enrolment office. The secretary was very helpful with my enrolment, and I was able to communicate in French as she spoke slowly and clearly. I was given forms to fill out, received my student card and told to check my subject selection with M. Ludwig.

I waited outside M. Ludwig's office and ten minutes after the appointed time he arrived. He was casually dressed and had thin hair that couldn't be described as tidy. He had a happy disposition and greeted me with a cheery "Bonjour!" I was glad I didn't know that M. Ludwig was a renowned academic in the field of the philosophy of science and the author of academic books and articles. I sat in his office and discussed my subjects. He was patient, spoke slowly and was very helpful. I wished to take an option called Atelier d'Ecriture (writing workshop) but thought it might be too difficult. He suggested I tackle it as it would be good experience. I decided to take this subject and sport as options.

I enjoyed my chat with M. Ludwig; he was pleasant and friendly and I felt welcome at the Sorbonne.

The next matter was my bag. I have carried a handbag for the last twenty-five years. I dislike bulky items in my pockets and I rarely wear a coat so any object I carried before using a handbag was deposited in my trouser pockets. It was very convenient, the only disadvantage being that I would sometimes leave the bag on the roof of my car and drive off without it.

Damien seemed to take a pathological dislike of my bag. He regaled me with stories of robberies on the streets of Paris and on the train. He constantly said, "You are being stupid. Why don't you get rid of that dilapidated old bag and buy a bag with a shoulder strap? Someone will snatch your bag and you will have to cancel your credit cards, you will lose your money."

I couldn't see the difference. If someone was prepared to snatch a bag from my arm, why not from my shoulder? But as I left M. Ludwig I thought about Damien and decided keeping the old bag was not worth the angst Damien was giving me.

Buying a bag, for me, was not a simple purchase. For a start I only wanted one bag. I didn't have a different bag for formal occasions, going to a sporting event or a casual dinner. One bag had to fit all. The bag had to be black leather, as small as possible and be able to fit my credit cards, cash, glasses, sunglasses and mobile phone. I went to Les Halles, a complex very like David Jones in Sydney, and after much searching found a bag to replace my old favourite.

I headed back to the apartment and as usual alighted at Gare de L'Est. I crossed the road and sat on the footpath. There was a typical row of buildings and I sat on the street with my back to the wall near a restaurant. I emptied the old bag of all my precious possessions and transferred them to the new black bag with its shiny black shoulder strap.

I put the new bag behind me. I was now sitting cross-legged on the footpath looking at Gare de L'est. I was wearing thongs, a T-shirt and my old jeans. I was attached to my old bag and sad to see it go. It lay open in front of me. I watched the passing parade. I was at peace with the world. I was happy. I was even happier when a young man walked past and dropped fifty cents into my bag.

Four

As far as I was able, I wanted to replicate the routines and activities I undertook in Sydney into my daily life in Paris. I believed that physical fitness was one of the keys to good health, particularly at my age. There were very few things that prevented me from exercising.

I have frequented gymnasiums spasmodically for most of my life. I would start a program, engage a personal trainer, religiously follow the program and then drop it. For the twelve months before I travelled to Paris, I trained at Fitness First in Miranda. My personal trainer was a young body builder, Chris Penfold. Before I engaged Chris, I looked in the mirror and saw a fat little man. The little was non-negotiable, but the fat was choice; I could fix the problem with exercise. The scales were my friend and I would weigh myself daily to make sure I didn't get fatter.

Chris was typical of all my personal trainers. The most important attribute of a personal trainer was the ability to bear pain. I trained with Chris three times a week and I was always in pain. I always had to lift that slightly heavier weight, row that little bit harder, pedal the bike a little faster.

Chris bore my pain with stoic indifference. I was making a significant contribution to paying his mortgage; I am sure that went some way to assuaging his pain.

I still remember when I first met Chris. After he agreed to train me, he told me his hourly rate—I later rang my bank to arrange an overdraft. Chris stood a metre in front of me. He looked me up and down, paused, and kindly said,

"You're old and overweight. You cannot exercise like a twenty-year-old. You will have to change your diet."

"How do you know what I eat and drink?"

"I'm not blind."

"I don't want to go on a diet," I said. "I want to lose weight with exercise."

"You don't need to lose weight. You need to reduce your fat and increase your muscle. Muscle is heavier than fat, so you won't appear so fat, but you may be heavier. Put the scales away, you don't need them."

"Are you going to give me a calorie counting diet?"

"Yes and no," Chris said. "You will eat as much as you want, but you will eat different things at different times of the day."

"I suppose sometime or other you will actually give me some exercises."

What appeared to be a cruel smile crossed his lips as he said, "I think that can be arranged."

He started the first session by cross-examining me regarding my eating habits. I disclosed details of the worst of Western society's eating habits. He made notes. He was very perspicacious. He suggested I reduce my coffee intake from four cappuccinos a day to two. Otherwise I could eat whatever I liked.

The exercises he introduced me to, at first, were not very strenuous. Chest presses, shoulder raises, leg lifts and so on were all familiar to me. I had three sessions a week and Chris wanted me to exercise on another three days. This exercise comprised walking for fifty minutes. It didn't matter how far, or how fast; it was just important that I actually moved.

Week after week passed and the exercises not only became harder, but more varied. I didn't understand what he was doing. I just did what he said. The exercises consisted of muscle building, lifting, to me, what were heavy weights. He gave me aerobic-type exercises; rowing and bike riding to improve my stamina. He noticed my posture was poor and my core strength lacking. The exercises were always hard and exhausting. He varied the exercises over time to meet my physiological needs which of course required considerable expertise. The overdraft was justified.

The biggest and most imperceptible change was to my diet. Chris spoke to me regularly during exercise sessions about what I ate. He suggested I buy a rice cooker and substitute basmatic rice for potato mashed in butter and cream. I had a huge advantage. A few years earlier I asked my wife, Josie, if she minded if I did the cooking. With some reluctance, she agreed. I enrolled in a basic knife skills class at the local community college as well as a couple of other cooking classes. This meant I could cook whatever I liked. Josie was a healthy eater and other than rarely eating meat, she was understanding and flexible.

Gradually, Chris' subtle manipulation changed my eating habits. He introduced me to the 'My Fitness Pal' app. I slowly changed my habits such that I consumed mainly carbohydrates at the beginning of the day and protein at night. My intake of vegetables and fish increased. I never became pedantic or fanatical but; every night, I ate twenty-one almonds before I went to bed.

Chris' technique was deceptively simple. Instead of attempting to radically change my diet he encouraged me to make small changes over a twelve-month period. In twelve months, my fat to body weight ratio dropped. Chris eschewed the body mass index test and used calipers to measure my actual fat. The Penfold method of incremental change meant each small adjustment to my daily food intake became permanent. Subtle changes revolutionised what I ate, every day.

In Paris the Penfold method of perpetual fitness and health was about to be tested. My eating habits were well ingrained, but I needed to find a gym before my motivation to exercise disappeared in the face of my study priorities.

I researched gymnasiums in Paris. The most convenient was Fitness First on Boulevarde St. Gemaine. It was housed in what appeared to be a historical building with a centuries-old façade of ornate carvings and columns decorating its exterior. The entrance occupied the entire front of the building. Beyond the wide glass doors were wide steps stretching upwards. I saw gates and lights, green and mainly red. At the top of the stairs was a counter that separated me from a young woman who smiled as I approached.

"I am in Paris for six months, can I look at the gym please?" I gave myself a pat on the back for being able to communicate in French.

She motioned me to walk through the gate and past the counter. I gazed at a row of treadmills, cheek by jowl, lining the wall. There was no other equipment in sight. The next level was the centre of the gym. Immediately in front of me was aerobic equipment with stationary bikes, rowing machines, pull-up bars, and the like. To the left, in a space separately delineated, was an area where heavy lifting occurred. I sniffed the air. I felt at home as a faint smell of liniment and sweat wafted past my nose. There was a bench press, leg press machine, free-weights and assorted other equipment. At the other end of the room was a small mat used for free exercises such as the plank, sit-ups, push-ups and other forms of torture. The men's change room consisted of about four rows of mahogany benches below mahogany lockers. It was spotlessly clean. The showers were numerous and very public. The gym by Australian standards was very small.

I unsuccessfully attempted to transfer my Fitness First membership in Australia to this gym so I reluctantly paid the significant membership fee for six months. My angst of having to pay two membership fees was alleviated by the knowledge that I no longer contributed to Chris Penfold's mortgage payments.

The gym was ideal. Although small, it had all the equipment I needed. Its main advantage was that it was five minutes walk from the university. I typically exercised before or after lunch when it was least crowded.

I decided to utilise the heavy weights section and soon become a regular. Each time I saw the same faces exercising, loitering in the change room or having a shower. Occasionally someone spoke English, however, in the main French was the sole language. I rarely spoke to anyone, I just did my thing. I had an exercise program. I put weights on the machine, did repetitions, rested, changed the weights, did repetitions. My fellow gym junkies, not that I was a junkie of course, were serious about exercise. During my rest periods, without asking, they jumped in, loaded my machine with weights, did their own repetitions, and after they finished, removed most of the weights so I could resume lifting. In this way we used the same equipment at the same time. I permitted this, not because they were huge men, but rather because I am, by nature, a sharing person.

* * *

In the course of the next couple of weeks I tried to familiarise myself with the transport system in Paris, but it was not easy.

Damien ensured that I settled in quickly. It was obvious that my sole means of transport in Paris would be train and bicycle. Damien met me at Gare de L'Est, and helped me obtain a Navigo pass. This was a pass that I topped up weekly in a machine at the station, and enabled me to travel on the Paris Metro, and access the Paris Velib system.

Paris had a system of bike stations, scattered throughout the city. A bike station consisted of a row of bikes, each bike, called a Velib, anchored to a metal post. Taking a bike was as simple as swiping the Navigo pass on a pad on the post. The bike was released and I was on my way. It didn't matter where I wanted to go in Paris, I was never far from a bike station.

There were dedicated bike lanes in Paris but unlike Sydney, or other cities, bike lanes in Paris were not the exclusive preserve of bikes. The lanes were shared with taxis and buses. The lanes were barely wide enough for a bus let alone a bus and a bike. I rode my bike from the 10th arrondissement where I lived and followed the canal toward the centre of the city. Suddenly a bus appeared inches from my shoulder and I was forced to ride in the gutter. Monks and meditation gurus speak of 'being present'. I was never present. I lived my life in dreams, and only responded to an immediate event, such as someone speaking to me. It would be years later after stints in hospital that meditation and being present would be crucial elements of my mental wellbeing. While cycling in Paris I learnt to be present, that is, be aware of my surroundings. I acquired an acute sense of awareness of diesel engines. I subconsciously became aware of a bus when it was fifty metres behind me. Being present was an essential element of riding a bike safely in Paris.

However, there were many roads in Paris that didn't have

bike lanes, and bikes just shared the road with traffic. It took me some time to understand the road rules that applied to bikes. I didn't have a set of road rules so I learnt by observation. This was entirely appropriate as a philosophy student at the Sorbonne; Aristotle postulated that humans, from a very early age, learnt by imitation or mimesis.

The first general rule that applied to motor vehicles related to pedestrian crossings. In Paris pedestrian crossings are places designed to gather pedestrians in the one place so that a number of people can be run down at the same time rather than just one at a time. Red, green and yellow lights all meant the same: proceed, unless to do so would result in an accident. One day I was riding on the street minding my own business, when I was pulled over by a very officious policewoman. I stopped and she yelled at me.

"Je ne comprends pas," I said.

She yelled louder, so I repeated what I said before. When she yelled even louder and added "c'est dangereux," I knew feigned ignorance wouldn't work, so I said sorry, turned the bike around and rode on the correct side of the road.

Paris was comparatively flat, and bike riding was popular; the usage of Velibs was enormous. One of the first things I noticed was that I was the slowest bike on the road. Everyone was overtaking me; in some streets there were very narrow, bike-only lanes, with a gutter on one side and a small concrete wall on the other—room for only one bike. I found it disconcerting to hear a bell behind me indicating someone wanted to overtake. I put my slowness down to the fact that everyone was much younger than me until one day a geriatric woman nonchalantly overtook me. Of course, at sixty-six years of age I was neither geriatric nor elderly.

I was fortunate that I didn't wish to pursue any woman on a bike. In ancient Greek mythology, Atalanta, a beautiful virgin, did a deal with her father who wanted to marry her off. If anyone wanted to marry her they had to beat her in a foot race. If they lost, she beheaded them. A mound of heads quickly formed. Melonian wanted to marry her so he sought outside help. Aphrodite gave him three golden apples. As Atalanta passed him he successively threw golden apples in front of her. She couldn't help herself. It was like throwing a stick to a dog. The moment she saw an apple, she chased it and picked it up. Melonian won the race and married her. My bike riding was so poor even if I had a sack full of golden apples I still wouldn't have beaten a geriatric woman. Just as well. After Atalanta and Melonian married, the gods turned them into lions. I would have been turned into a pussycat, but I wanted to be a dolphin; an intelligent animal that enjoyed a good time and had no natural enemies.

As my fitness improved my speed also improved. The bike was a great way to travel. I could walk fifty metres to the nearest Velib station, choose a bike and cycle to my next destination. On arrival, I lodged the bike into the station close to my destination. In this way, I cycled the length of the Canal Saint Matin, visited the Eiffel Tower, Notre-Dame, the Arc de Triomphe, various gymnasiums and markets. There were no parking issues, no traffic jams. It was a perfect way to travel. Of course, if the weather was fine.

The arrangement I had with Damien was that I paid him a weekly sum and in return I had exclusive use of a bedroom and shared use of bathroom, toilet, kitchen and lounge room. He provided all my food, and cooked three evening meals a week. All other meals, I prepared myself. The only television set was in the lounge room.

I didn't instinctively like Damien, nor did I dislike him. I had a roof over my head, excellent study facilities, so nothing else mattered. Meals with Damien were in the kitchen. We ate together on the three nights he cooked for me. The kitchen was a tiny corridor. I walked through the doorway (there was no room for a door) and observed on the right wall a pantry, refrigerator, sink, dishwasher below a small bench, and hot plates with cupboards below. There wasn't an oven. On the left-hand wall was a small space then a small table with two chairs that backed on to a cupboard that held cutlery, crockery and a small bench. It was impossible for two people to be in the cooking area at the same time. At the end of the kitchen was a tiny balcony. This balcony was used to store non-perishable food items. Every nook and cranny in the kitchen was occupied. There was an abundance of food in the refrigerator and pantry.

I enjoyed cooking, and had attended a course at TAFE that specialised in desserts. Wednesday evening back at home had become a favourite day for the children who lived next door. I didn't eat crème brulee, chocolate mousse, panna cotta, tiramisu, lime and liquorice parfait, croquembouche and so on because these desserts were unhealthy, full of sugar and cream. Hypocritically, every Wednesday after TAFE, I was happy to give my desserts to the young children next door to enjoy. I resolved, even though I had learned to love cooking, that I wouldn't cook in Damien's kitchen.

About a week after I arrived we were sitting in the kitchen. Damien asked me what I did for a living. I mentioned that I had been a practising lawyer for over twenty years. I should have known better. The minute I told someone that I practised law, I was either specifically asked a legal question or regaled about previous grave injustices perpetrated by the legal system. Damien was no exception.

He was currently involved in bitter divorce proceedings with his wife, and was estranged from his only son. He ear-bashed me with stories of his protracted divorce proceedings, and told of his hatred of a greedy manipulative wife. Apparently, all was well with the marriage until his wife decided she would have a social life for which she needed money that he was not willing to supply. In addition to the divorce proceedings he had a legal battle with his only sibling, an estranged sister, over the distribution of their parents' estate. Damien railed against his son Romain, an indolent young man who sponged off him, and refused to study. It went in one ear and out the other.

I was very unhappy with the conversation. Damien always spoke in English. I attempted to answer in French, however I felt Damien made it difficult. He knew I was a student, knew I was undertaking a difficult university course, and it was blindingly obvious my language skills were poor. Damien was the only person I met in Paris who refused to help me improve my French. My resentment of Damien's topics of conversation was exacerbated by his insistence on speaking in English. Our failure to communicate in French prejudiced my attitude towards him, to the extent that I failed to appreciate the help and kindness he often showed.

Just before university was due to start, I noticed Damien inside the restaurant I first noticed when I arrived at Gare de L'Est. It was mid-morning and I was coming back from the gym, so on the spur of the moment, I decided to have a cup of coffee with him. He was sitting at a small table near the door, so I sat down and ordered a flat white coffee. I remarked that I had never seen him there before. He told me that he had an argument with the previous owners and had not been in the restaurant for over twelve months. I commented that it must have been a serious dispute. My instinct was correct. With his two dogs sitting at his feet, Damien told me the story.

He began by describing the barman who served him twelve months ago as stupid and unreasonable. Damien had come into the restaurant with his two dogs, to have a coffee.

"One of the dogs had an accident," Damien said.

"You mean it pissed on the floor?" I said.

"It was an accident. The barman was very rude. If he would have given me a mop I would have cleaned it up."

I was intrigued by Damien's calm manner. I wondered if I didn't fully understand French culture. I had never seen a dog in a restaurant in Cronulla, let alone see a dog 'have an accident' in a restaurant. I thought that the barman had every right to be rude and in Australia Damien and his dogs would be sitting on the footpath in a flash. I resisted the temptation to note that having dogs in restaurants was unhealthy and to have a dog piss on the floor pretty gross.

"A week later I went into the restaurant to have lunch. I was right in the middle of lunch when the dog had an accident."

"You mean another one?"

"Yes," he replied. "The dog had an accident on a tourist's suitcase. I was very nice about it, and I told the barman I was quite happy to have the suitcase cleaned, even though it was an accident."

I could barely contain my laughter, but I had a sense of unease. Damien's speech was very matter-of-fact about the incident. It was as if a dog having an accident was quite normal, and should be accepted by the waiter as if it was a young child whose lack of toilet training was normal, and should be tolerated. The impact on other diners and the tourist, of a dog urinating in an eating area seemed lost on Damien. I put this egocentric behaviour into the back of my mind as something I must accommodate in our unavoidable interactions.

"The barman told me I must leave the restaurant immediately. I refused to go until I finished my lunch. After all, anyone, even a dog can have an accident. The next day I was walking past the restaurant when the barman came into the street, and started to abuse me. I punched him in the nose. The police were called and I had to go to court. All because of a stupid ignorant barman."

The casual reference to his preparedness to inflict physical violence surprised me, and I was disconcerted by it. Even more disconcerting was the emotionless way the event was described—I worried that it indicated embryonic psychopathic tendencies.

Unfortunately, Damien's dogs were quite accident-prone. I had noticed accidents in my bedroom and in the hallway and had intended to take this up with Damien. As I listened to his story I decided not to discuss dogs and accidents with him. It was wiser to keep the bedroom door shut.

It became customary for us to have a discussion in the kitchen three nights a week over dinner. Damien cooked to a fixed menu that he dictated. Luckily I had no allergies, and there wasn't any food I disliked. He cooked a variety of food including offal, pasta, vegetables but never red meat or egg-based dishes. Tonight's menu was lambs fry with bacon and mashed potatoes, followed by chocolate ice cream washed down with coffee. Our topic of discussion was homelessness. I had noticed that the same people sat every day on the footpaths near the apartment. Damien concurred and recounted his interaction with the homeless.

A few months earlier, a homeless man camped within one hundred metres of Damien's apartment. By camped, Damien meant that the man spent his days in lonely solitude staring into nothing. Damien regularly walked his dogs past the homeless man every day without acknowledgement. One day the dogs ran up to the man and licked him on the face. The man pushed them away, initially with his hands, then with his feet. I would have done the same. I liked dogs but I hate being licked in the face. Damien didn't suggest that the man hurt the dogs. While he was telling this story, he got up, went to a cupboard and pulled out a can of capsicum spray.

He said, "You can own this in France but you're not allowed to use it."

He told me that after the man pushed the dogs away he returned home, picked up the capsicum spray, returned to where the homeless man was sitting, and sprayed him with the capsicum spray. The man hurried away, and never returned.

Dogs had a sacred role in ancient Egyptian religion. They were associated with Anubis, the jackal-headed god of the underworld. Given Damien's behaviour the association between dogs and the underworld was very apt. His attitude in the restaurant when he excused the unpleasant behaviour of his dogs and assaulted the barman combined worshipping dogs with criminality. To facilitate my survival, I decided to regard Damien's dogs as sacred.

Damien worked for IBM and appeared to have flexible working hours. Occasionally I came home, and walked into the lounge room to see a young man sitting on the lounge. Damien introduced me to Pierre, his 'work' colleague. Pierre was friendly, approachable, and always spoke to me in French. He was tall and thin with a full head of hair, and softly spoken. Damien was less loquacious in his presence, and spoke to him quite softly. I instinctively didn't trust Damien's description of him as a work colleague. I had no reason to doubt Damien's word except that he seemed to relate differently to Pierre than he did to me. There was a way he looked at him, staring for some time with a slight smile on his face, that I had yet to see between work colleagues.

Three weeks into my stay, Damien announced that we were having guests for dinner. The guests were Damien's son Romain, and Pierre. It was a relief that I would have contact with others, and perhaps even speak French. After listening to Damien's robust criticism of his son I was somewhat surprised that Romain was a dinner guest. I had assumed, incorrectly, that they were estranged.

Romain opened the door to the apartment with his own key, and entered without knocking or fanfare. He was a slim young man, about twenty years of age. He sat at the table exuding the exuberance of youth. Damien greeted him with a hug, and offered him a drink before introducing him to me. Damien was smiling and cheerful, and fussed over him, asking after his girlfriend and his studies. Pierre arrived shortly after. Romain, Pierre and Damien greeted each other in French. Pierre and myself exchanged greetings, and at Damien's direction we sat at the dining table squeezed into the corner of the lounge room.

"Je veux seulement parlais Francaise, s'il vous plait," I said.

Romain and Pierre spoke only in French. When I didn't understand something they patiently repeated themselves. They listened to my attempts to speak French with understanding and interest. Damien spoke in French to Pierre and Romain and spoke to me in English. Romain had a girlfriend who would be soon leaving for China. Pierre told me Romain was very popular with girls. It was not difficult to see why. Not only was he a good-looking young man, he was absolutely charming. I found it hard to reconcile this fine young man with the layabout Damien railed about on my first night, but I would soon learn that there were many things hard to reconcile about Damien. In previously describing Romain, Damien spoke of chalk. I met, and discovered cheese. Our dialogue was very stilted given my language limitations, and our discussion was slow, but if they found it tedious they disguised their feelings. They assisted my conversation, judiciously helped with an English word when my French vocabulary completely failed. We talked about what it was like to live in Australia, how many children I had and what they were like. Pierre wanted to discuss Australian wines, of which I knew little. I used to teach geography so I explained the climatic conditions in the Barossa Valley and the Hunter Region in New South Wales. Romain was particularly interested in my family situation in that I had two children from different marriages. He quizzed me about my relationship with my first wife. In simple language, I explained that my divorce was amicable and court orders were not required to resolve property, maintenance or custody issues. I used many words to say simple things, and I noticed for the first time Damien was glowering. I suspected my experience contrasted unfavourably with the bitter antagonism that existed between Damien and his estranged wife. The evening passed very quickly and I enjoyed Romain and Pierre's company. Romain offered to take me shopping.

Five

I had three weeks before my classes officially started at the end of September, so I started to explore where I would be studying. My favourite place in Paris was the Latin Quarter at St. Michel. The exit to the station at St. Michel spewed commuters onto the footpath next to the ubiquitous French restaurant. The exit I used was at Place St. Michel. It was not really a 'place' but an area where a number of boulevards converged.

Very close, but not visible, was the Seine, a working river. At this point it was a narrow concrete canal. Sometimes I sat on the edge of the wall and watched commercial barges, recreational craft and tourist boats move slowly through the canal.

Wide boulevards ran adjacent to the river. The buildings on the side of the boulevards were separated by the boulevards and, of course, the river. There was considerable distance between the rows of buildings. The buildings, no more than seven storeys high, consisted mainly of apartments. These apartments with their tiny Juliette balconies, stained pale brown and grey by pollution, had a sense of timelessness, an historical beauty.

Like much of Paris there was a surprising amount of vegetation. Mature trees were common in this area. The relatively low-rise buildings, wide spaces and trees created an ambience of space.

The traffic was horrendous. There was a constant roar of engines, of cars stopping, starting and accelerating. The contradiction was obvious. The tranquility of the visual competed with the pollution of noise. It was almost as obvious as my life. I was enjoying the variation, the freedom, the experiences that contradicted the difficulty I would have achieving my goal of passing all subjects at the Sorbonne.

Ten metres from the station exit at Place St. Michel was Rue de la Huchette. Twenty metres along Rue de La Huchette, it bent to the left; spearing off to the right was Rue de la Harpe. These rues bent and turned, others such as Rue St. Severine and Rue Xavier Privas diverged. They were narrow and were either brick paved or had a concave concrete surface with a drain in the middle. Footpaths didn't exist. This area was a maze to wander through, to lose a sense of direction, to retrace steps, to enjoy.

The rues were always crowded, bounded on both sides with places to eat. The food was as diverse as the nationalities of the tourists. I observed cuisine Francaise, Francaise Provencal, Morrocan, Greek, vegetarian, Lebanese, pizza, Oriental, and Indian. There were bars, restaurants, simple food, complex food, take away food and a small cinema. There was a sense of crowded intimacy. The businesses on the edge of the rues were beneath seven-storey buildings. Juliette balconies jutted from the side of buildings, dilapidated apartments stretching to the sky blocking the sun and appearing to further narrow the rues. The rues, occupied by happy meandering crowds and devoid of traffic, provided a refuge from the frenetic activity of the city.

I had just finished a gym session and was looking to eat. I passed L'Auberge Moulin, advertised as a traditional French restaurant. At the entrance to the restaurant was a very overweight, slightly balding, middle-aged man. He sported a large handlebar moustache and wore a beret and traditional rural French apron. I looked at him with contempt. His pseudo-traditional French garb was a tacky attempt to entice gullible tourists—hawkers stood outside most of the restaurants, seeking to entice passersby in to eat.

I noticed the menu contained boeuf bourguignon, a beef stew with red wine sauce, rich in protein, the best type of meal after a gym workout. I wandered through the maze, up and down, deciding what to eat. I walked up and down, round and about for twenty minutes, looking at all possibilities. Boeuf bourguignon was my meal of choice. Reluctantly, I returned to the imposter whom I thought of as Porky.

I stepped down into the restaurant and Porky showed me to my table. The restaurant was dark. It had a low ceiling, stone walls with dull yellow lamps on them and on a pillar in the middle of the restaurant. Small, dull red lamps flickered on the made-up tables. I looked at the menu and noticed a handwritten addition. Lapin Spaghetti. I loved rabbit but had never had it with spaghetti. Spaghetti didn't meet my dietary requirements but the opportunity to eat rabbit took priority. I decided on half a dozen snails as an entrée, with baked apple as dessert. A glass of red wine and a café crème would make an adequate lunch.

There was a delay. I didn't like speaking in French and being answered in English. I was trying hard to pronounce

French words accurately. I sat and thought. I must be speaking French with an English accent. I postulated that it related to the tone of my voice and inflection. I silently practised, before Porky took my order.

I practised a guttural way of speaking, as if I was permanently clearing my throat. Instead of emphasising the first syllable of a word, as in English, I practised emphasising subsequent syllables.

I turned my attention to the words on the menu. Porky arrived to take my order.

I ordered. "EscGARGO, lapUN (with the 'n' silent), pomme a four exactEment. Je voudRais bordEAUZ vin piCHET."

Porky reached on to my table, picked up the glass, and said, "So you want a glass of wine?"

When the food arrived, I was not disappointed. Snails were usually only served in French restaurants in Sydney. I am partial to oysters and the texture of oysters and snails were quite similar, oysters being slimier. I extracted the dozen snails, cooked in a garlic herb butter, from their shells with a narrow two-pronged fork. I enjoyed it, although there was no difference between the snails (escargot) at the L'Aberge Moulin and at café Sel and Poivre in Darlinghurst.

To me, rabbit was a delicacy, to everyone else it seemed to be poison. Perhaps I thought it was a delicacy because I was such a poor shot that I could never order rabbit for dinner when I stayed at Hill End. I always enjoyed things I wasn't supposed to have, or the things I couldn't have, more than things that came easily to me. The rabbit was texturally delicate with quite a strong flavour. I was glad I was seduced into entering the restaurant.

A week later, after exercising I decided to eat. I decided that snails, beef stew and baked apple would be an ideal meal after lifting weights. I walked to L'Auberge Moulin. It was very cold. Porky was inside. He greeted me with a big smile and a welcoming laugh. I walked to the same table. I was a creature of habit.

He pulled out a chair and laughed again.

"La table de semaine derniere."

He knew my table. He patted me on the shoulder and gave me a menu. I noticed his demeanour. He was very attentive to his customers. He obviously got joy from looking after people. I ordered through another waiter.

The meal arrived. I had the newspaper open in front of me; I was reading the dictionary trying to understand the difference between prevenir and parvenir. Wearing the same apron and beret, he said, "Desole," and moved the paper to put the snails in front of me. Another smile, a pat on the shoulder and "bon appetite" and I was ready to eat.

I was now unaware of his costume. I was occupying my space and he was occupying his space. Our spaces overlapped and we were influencing each other. It was always the way. I had initially entered the restaurant out of necessity. His friendly good humour and genuine care for me, a customer, made me see him differently. He was no longer the charlatan enticing me into his restaurant with faux tradition. He was no longer overweight but a favourite uncle, and I was not eating at a restaurant; I was at home.

Enticing people into a restaurant when there was a multitude of competition was difficult. On another day, I turned into Rue Xavier Privas. It was the narrowest rue and appeared to have the most eating places and certainly the most hawkers. I noticed groups of people strolling along. A young hawker was having extraordinary success in persuading people to enter his restaurant. I recognised the technique immediately; the same utilised by a real estate agent based in Cronulla, whose name was Greg Gilbert. It was uncanny. He looked like Greg Gilbert and had similar mannerisms. This young man, obviously very good, must have sat at the feet of Greg Gilbert, the master.

I first met Greg in the mid-eighties. He was in partnership with another agent John Quinn. Greg was a man of bulk, with a round face and a prominent nose. His unusual laugh dominated his personality. He looked very suave in his light-coloured fawn suit, and he never sat still, was always moving to the next deal, thinking of the next sale, the next opportunity.

Greg's big advantage was his training. He was a curtain salesman. There couldn't be a more fitting training for a real estate salesman. Imagine a room with a very large floor-to-ceiling picture window. The room had tables, antique chairs and on one wall stood a fireplace with a stone wall set above it. The stone had a large crack in it. One wall had paint that had peeled. Parts of the timber floor were stained. Bright sunlight shone into the room. The truth of the room was there for all to see. Curtains were then strategically partially drawn across the window. The curtains hid the crack in the stone and threw shadows on the stains in the floor. The bright light was now concentrated on the antique furniture and the cleverly painted mural on the other wall. There was now a different truth. Greg didn't know it, but he was a philosopher. He would've liked Nietzsche. Nietzsche observed, "There are no facts, only interpretations."

I was looking for an entry-level waterfront when I first met Greg. An entry-level waterfront is a run-down dump with acres of mud in front of it at low tide. John Quinn, Greg's partner, showed me a waterfront property in Port Hacking. John described it as almost derelict and beyond repair. The detailed inspection with his expert commentary convinced me that buying the property would be a mistake. He then showed me another property that he considered much better value. That same afternoon I walked into their office. Greg was alone and I asked if he had any properties to show me. I jumped into his car and we headed for an inspection. Greg showed me an absolute bargain. He assured me it was unique. It was in need of some repair but with a lick of paint, upgrading of bathrooms and perhaps a new kitchen I would have a dream waterfront. Greg did not appear to see the rotting timber, leaking roof, and missing gutters. It was the same house John had showed me that morning. When John showed me the property there were no curtains on the windows. Greg strategically drew the curtains.

Of course, Greg's philosophy was right. Real estate was not about facts or truth, it was about interpretations that made money or bought dreams. I trusted Greg. Through Greg, I bought and sold properties that made me money and realised my dream.

The young man outside the French restaurant plied his trade. Like Greg he had no inhibitions. He was prepared to talk to anyone at any time. Engaging with the passing parade of people was second nature. People were walking, looking and talking. His first task was to stop them and engage them. Other hawkers had the same task. The typical engagement was:

"Bonjour, do you want to eat?"

The hawker showed the menu and the reply was usually, "No thanks."

The Greg Gilbert lookalike had a different approach.

He picked his mark. When someone ambling past glanced in his direction he said, "I have a free glass of wine, especially for you."

The critical words were 'free' and 'special'. The word 'free' was an appeal to basic human greed. We all wanted something for nothing. Even though we knew that nothing was free, that there was always a cost, a trade-off. When something was free we were less inclined to analyse the cost.

The word 'special' meant different things to different people. We all like to think we are special. The connotation was that the person had been identified as being unique and as such was being offered the gift. On the spur of the moment the word 'special' was absorbed subconsciously. To our Greg lookalike the person was in fact special. He was special to him because if he ate at the restaurant money was made.

Few people resisted the initial approach. This allowed the menu to be sold. Magnificent traditional French cuisine, very cheap, would provide a gastronomic experience not possible anywhere else. The tone was friendly and firm; how could anyone resist the opportunity being presented. More times than not, people he targeted followed him into the restaurant. After the kill, I noticed the confident swagger and the barely perceptible smirk that came with the triumph of a sale. I had seen it before.

I decided to eat. I didn't need the sales pitch. I was curious to compare the promise to the reality. The waiter showed me to a table and immediately placed a glass of water in front of me. This committed me to the table and ensured that I couldn't leave. The free glass of wine arrived. It was a tiny glass filled with cheap French wine. I ordered poulet fermier sauté au vinaigre. It was passable, but hardly a gastronomic delight.

Greg Gilbert was unique in that he did not need passing trade. If no one walked past the Greg Gilbert lookalike he didn't sell anything. The real Greg Gilbert had no such handicap. Greg Gilbert was able to sell property that was not for sale.

Greg had a gift. He had the uncanny ability to park himself inside my head. I *thought* I knew what I wanted, Greg *knew* what I wanted.

Josie and I bought a knock-down waterfront property in Dolans Bay. We were about to start building a new home when one Saturday morning there was a knock at the door.

Greg strolled in, his usual suave self in his fawn suit and half smile.

Josie walked into the kitchen, baby and toddler in tow and made us coffee. After some chit-chat, Greg made his announcement.

"I have come to tell you you're moving."

Josie and I looked at each other and smiled. Our smiles said we knew that Greg was up to something.

"I suppose you wouldn't mind sharing with us where we're moving to."

"Woolooware Road. The inspection's in an hour."

"We can't afford to own two properties," Josie said. "We've just bought this one."

"That's okay—I have a solicitor who will buy this house."

An hour later, Josie, myself and two kids were looking at a house in Woolooware Road, Burraneer. We parked on the street and walked down a curved driveway with pine trees lining the edges of the drive. Josie had come along for the ride. Then and thirty years later, Josie was the same. She didn't need or want a big house. She regularly visited the hairdresser but only occasionally had manicures or pedicures. We were at times poor and at times wealthy. It didn't matter; Josie was the horticulturist, child carer, financial manager, home economist, wife and mother. The only jewellery she ever asked for was an engagement and wedding ring.

There was a tennis court beyond the trees and a gazebo covered in wisteria in full bloom. A small three-bedroomed cottage stood behind the tennis court. The main house was a magnificent two-storey residence. Its pale orange painted exterior was covered in red and purple bougainvillea. Past the house a courtyard with a magnificent gum tree led to a large kidney-shaped swimming pool directly overlooking the deep waterfront to Burraneer Bay. The deep waterfront had a boathouse, and jetty to accommodate a large cruiser.

The interior matched the exterior. Huge double doors opened into a foyer. The foyer led to a magnificent lounge room and separate dining room, each opening via French doors onto a large balcony overlooking the bay. The bedrooms and bathrooms were upstairs.

The main bedroom entrance door faced windows that looked onto the tennis court. On the same wall was a hidden entrance to the walk-in robe and bathroom. The feature of the room was the bed. It was a king-size bed sitting on a platform. Three steps led up to base of the bed set against the wall with four posts. A facia board and drapes connected to the posts. King Henry VIII would have been very comfortable, even in agony from gout, lying on this bed.

Josie climbed on to the bed, sat on the mattress, and issued a startled cry. I went to look. In the ceiling above the bed was a mirror reflecting the whole of the bed. Josie was aghast. I couldn't see the problem; I looked like Danny Devito and my friends said, in being with Josie, that I was punching way above my weight.

As we walked down the drive after inspecting the property Josie looked at me apprehensively.

"You're not thinking of buying this, are you? We can't afford it." I sensed the alarm in her voice.

"We can afford it, and I am going to buy it."

"Well, if you think I'm going to sleep with you in that bed

in the main bedroom, with a mirror like that, you can think again."

"Ok, I will fix it as soon as we move in," I said.

Six weeks later we moved into the property and a solicitor bought our existing house. The first thing I did, being true to my word, was to deal with the mirror in the main bedroom.

I carried a high stepladder and all the equipment I needed into the bedroom. I climbed the stairs to the base of the bed and put the ladder on the base. I carefully climbed the ladder and sat on the top.

I polished the mirror.

A couple of days later I was awakened by the sound of tennis balls being hit on the tennis court. I wandered downstairs in my pyjamas, walked to the tennis court and saw Greg pick up a tennis ball about to serve. He saw me and said, "Just thought we'd have a hit."

"That's fine." I smiled, turned around and walked back into the house. I didn't mind—he obviously needed the practice.

Josie, myself and our two daughters settled into our new home. It wasn't long before we had an extensive social network. The focal point of the home was the tennis court. Josie had never played tennis before, but through sheer necessity she learnt. She quickly established a wider social network that centred on tennis. Every week, days were spent with mothers and their young children, sitting in the cabana, eating snacks and playing tennis. Through this network, I became involved with neighbours. Playing tennis, water skiing, eating in each other's houses, going to restaurants and shows together. The property was our home, the centre of our lives, the basis of our social acceptance, our happiness.

The three-bedroom house at the back of the tennis court housed two sisters, who lived rent-free in return for cooking, and looking after the children.

At the end of the year we held a tennis party; all the regular players and other friends came to our house with food and drink. The huge downstairs entertainment area converted to a dance venue, while outside, people lounged around the floodlit pool overlooking the river. Christmas lights hung from the huge gum tree that dominated the area between our home and the pool. Charity functions, Liberal Party functions and staff Christmas parties came and went in the four years we lived there.

I borrowed a lot of money to buy the property, originally a twenty-five-year principal and interest loan from the Advance Bank. I wanted to save money, so I changed from a principal and interest loan with Advance Bank to an interest-only loan with the Government Insurance Office (GIO). The catch was that I had to repay the GIO loan in full in three years instead of a twenty-five-year mortgage with the Advance Bank. I expected that at the end of three years, either the GIO would extend the loan for a further period or another bank, such as the Advance Bank, would refinance the loan. As it turned out my optimism was misplaced. After I had the loan for just over two years, the 'recession Australia had to have' hit. I knew I wasn't going to be able to pay off the loan in the agreed time, so six months before the loan to the GIO expired, I asked the GIO if they would extend my loan. They refused. I approached other banks but financial institutions weren't lending money. I was worried that in six months time I wouldn't be able to pay the GIO so I made the tough decision to sell the house. Within four months Wayne Gardner, world motorcycle champion, agreed to buy my house for two million dollars more than I paid for it. An appointment was made for the contracts to be exchanged on a Monday. The weekend before the exchange, Wayne attended an auction of a property nearby, owned by my friend

Geoff Bush, and without having previously seen it, bought it and not mine. My opportunity to repay the GIO loan vanished. The GIO demanded I repay my loan. I couldn't, so we had to negotiate a solution.

I wanted the property to be marketed by Greg Gilbert, under the control of the GIO. At that time waterfront houses on the Burraneer peninsular were usually sold without publicity, with multiple properties changing hands, sometimes with delayed settlement. Greg Gilbert was an expert in doing these deals. I believed once a mortgagee became publicly involved, the price would plummet.

I met the General Manager of the GIO in his office. Brian, an avuncular man in his mid-forties with a protruding stomach, rocked back on his chair as I entered his office. I was under no illusions as to my predicament. I was not a person with a wife and children, I was a problem, numbers in red ink on a profit and loss and balance sheet. My only hope was to align my interests with the GIO's interest.

"You haven't paid us so Mike Slag is going to sell your property," he said. This didn't make sense to me. I knew Mike, he was a GIO credit manager, familiar with defaulting car loans, but totally inexperienced in dealing with million-dollar properties.

"I don't think Mike can do the job. I have just as much to lose as you have if the sale is botched. I want an experienced local agent to market the property. Once there is a mortgagee sale, we will all lose."

"I couldn't care less. You say you've tried to sell it—you couldn't, I'm not about to trust you, or any of your cronies. Either pay us the money, or we'll sell it from under you," he declared as he dismissed me from his office. I was upset by his arrogance and offensive demeanour, but more upset by the fact I knew he was making a commercially poor decision that adversely affected me. My powerlessness distressed me, my future lay solely in the hands of others.

And so it passed. The GIO obtained default judgement for the debt, and obtained a writ of possession. I agreed to leave the property before the writ of possession was to be executed.

A week before we were to leave the property, Mike arrived at my doorstep, unannounced in the middle of the day. I happened to be home. I invited him inside and made Josie, Mike and myself a cup of tea. He wanted to know details of our move. I told him we would be moving next week, and even though I didn't have to, told him we had agreed to rent Wayne Gardner's house. Mike left the house. Our four-year-old daughter Mel was playing outside.

I heard sobbing, and Mel rushed into the kitchen. "That man said we're moving. I don't want to move, I want to stay here," she wailed. I was outraged.

"What did the man say?"

"When did mummy say you're moving?" she cried, very upset.

We hadn't as yet told our children about the adventure to our new house. I rushed down the drive to 'discuss' with Slag his conversation with my child. I saw his car disappear in the distance.

We moved into Wayne Gardner's house. I had no money. Geoff Bush, having sold the house to Wayne, wanted to rent it back from its new owner. Geoff was a divorcee and I had been best man at a couple of his weddings. Wayne's house had five bedrooms, and Geoff suggested we share the rent. The rent was seven hundred and fifty dollars, of which Geoff asked me to pay two hundred and fifty dollars. It was a gift to a friend in financial difficulties.

The GIO entered into possession after we moved house. Shortly afterwards, one Saturday, I went back to the property to remove some of my possessions from the boathouse. I was there for about an hour and while walking up from the waterfront I heard voices. I walked past the pool and saw a party in full swing. People were playing tennis, chatting, sitting in the cabana, men drinking beer, woman drinking wine, and young children playing around the garden. I was spotted by a man I knew as a senior executive of the GIO.

"What's going on?" I asked, as he approached.

"What do you mean? What do you think you're doing here?" he scowled.

"I'm clearing out stuff. You can't use my property," I said.

"Yes we can, this place is owned by the GIO, and you'd better piss off before I call the police."

"This is my home," I said.

"Piss off."

I quickly left. I was not afraid of confrontation; I didn't want him to see the tears in my eyes.

Sure enough, it wasn't long before the mortgagee signs were displayed. A double-page spread in the *Sutherland Shire Leader*, and hundreds of people trooping through the house. The sale appeared in Jonathan Chancellor's Title Deeds column in the Saturday *Sydney Morning Herald*, and just in case it was missed the first time, he repeated it. This was particularly humiliating. Chancellor's column specialised in displaying the misfortune of so-called 'high fliers'. He falsely tied my mortgagee sale to a so-called failed hospital project, which simply wasn't true. It made me look like a double loser. The property sold for more than I paid for it, but the GIO butchered the sale. The GIO had every right to sell the property, I agreed to pay them back, and didn't. I didn't deserve sympathy—I made a commercial decision to borrow the money, and had to live with the consequences of that decision. I borrowed the money in good faith and tried to repay it. I didn't deserve the humiliation, disrespect and indignity heaped upon me. It added to our sense of loss. It was our home, we lost the centre of our existence, our social networks collapsed. Friendships weakened, ended and in some cases strengthened. Circumstances changed, so people around me changed for better or worse. The mortgagee sale struck at my raison d'etre, what it meant to be a husband and father, the need to support and protect my family. I was a failure. The fact was that I made the mistakes and was caught up in the hubris of living in a grand waterfront estate. I didn't do it for my family. Josie was always happy, no matter where we were. I couldn't blame the GIO. Life was about choices, and I had to live with the choices I made.

I chose to study at the Sorbonne. To make a choice we need to exercise wisdom, which usually means understanding alternative choices and consequences. It is difficult to be wise if the consequences cannot be foreseen. If I had known what I faced, wisdom would have decreed that I stay home.

Six

It was my first day at the Sorbonne, and I was excited at the prospect of finally starting lectures. I was nervous, just as I was when I started at Sydney University fifty years earlier. I caught the Metro to Saint Germaine, and walked to the Sorbonne. I had a student log-in, my timetable, and I knew the location of each lecture and tutorial. The Sorbonne was very well organised.

I walked through the gate, showed my student identity card to the disbelieving security guard, and looked for the lecture hall. I walked down the same corridors that I had traversed a month earlier, looking for my lecture room. There was no room or lecture theatre that remotely resembled the lecture hall details on my timetable. In desperation, I approached students and asked in French where the lecture theatre was. I also asked if they spoke English. None of the people I approached knew the location of the lecture theatre, nor did they speak, or were prepared to speak, English.

I widened my search through the university and eventually found an administration office. I knew as soon as I entered the room that I had to communicate in French. I approached a woman sitting just inside the door and asked where the lecture theatre was. She appeared confused by my request.

"Je ne comprend pas."

I repeated my question.

"Je ne sais pas."

I had a stroke of genius. I asked her if I could use her 'ordinateur' (computer). Very reluctantly she acceded to my request. I logged in to the Sorbonne intranet that showed my timetable and the location of my lectures. I didn't understand French very well and the secretary spoke very slowly, with a wry smile on her face. Uncommonly, for a French person in an administrative position there was even a slight hint of sympathy.

"You are at the wrong university," she said.

"Excuse me, can you repeat that please."

"You are at the wrong university."

"That's impossible! I am enrolled at the Sorbonne."

"You are enrolled at Sorbonne IV, this University is Sorbonne III."

I was astonished. "Where is Sorbonne IV?"

"At Port Clingancourt." She took a map from her drawer and showed me where the university was in relation to the Metro station. I picked up her map, memorised the route, promptly forgot it, and handed it back.

This was a most inauspicious start to my studies at the Sorbonne; I was deflated. I now had to find Port Clingancourt. I always carried a Metro map and a road map of Paris. I retrieved the Metro map. A map of the Paris Metro rail system was akin to looking at spaghetti on a plate. The strands of spaghetti crossed each other, changed direction and intertwined from one edge of the plate to the other. Each strand of spaghetti had a different colour. Finding an individual Metro station on the map was rather like finding an ice-cream in my refrigerator after a visit from my grandchildren. I had a stroke of luck. Port Clingancourt and St. Germaine were on the same line, Line 4, coloured red on the map. That morning I walked to Gare de L'Est to catch the Metro on Line 4 towards the centre of Paris. In the future, I would walk to Gare de L'Est to travel in precisely the opposite direction, about the same distance, to Port Clingancourt at the end of Line 4.

I alighted from the train at Port Clingancourt and headed towards where I thought the university was situated. I walked upstairs at the end of the platform and onto a footpath outside a large restaurant. There was a narrow rue in front of me with a row of stationary buses. There were at least five possible roads I could take. I took a punt and followed some young people I hoped were students.

I followed the road and turned right towards the university. I walked down a pedestrian area with a couple of footpaths and large grass area. The pedestrian area was a safe passage removed from traffic. A narrow road was on my left. The start of the road bounded a construction site. I walked past the construction site to the 'sandstone' university in which I was enrolled. I only knew it was the university because there was a sign on the side of the building.

My first impression of the university building was that it was prefabricated. The first part of the building was raised and two storeys high. The façade had windows that resembled lookout positions in a castle, or perhaps it housed snipers in World War II. The second part was a multi-storey building with prefabricated sheeting and prominent vertical windows. I saw metal staircases behind the windows. The building was grey concrete. The Sorbonne was not what I imagined.

I entered the building and quickly located the lecture hall for my four o'clock lecture. I had time on my hands so

I decided to find the rooms where my tutorials would be held. The tutorials were on the fourth floor. Most of my time would be spent on the fourth floor. I was about to press the button for the lift when I noticed a sign that told me that students were not permitted to use the lift so I walked forty stairs to the fourth floor. I didn't consider this as exercise but a pain. There was no concession for the old (me) or, for that matter, the disabled.

My first lecture was the History of the Philosophy of Science, delivered by Pascal Ludwig. It was a typical university lecture. M. Ludwig lectured behind a lectern with a whiteboard behind him. Hundreds of students faced him in tiered rows looking down on him. He was just as I found him when I enrolled; good-humoured. I tried to take notes but soon gave up; taking notes of gibberish was pointless. The two-hour lecture exceeded my concentration span by about an hour and a quarter.

I was early when I arrived for the lecture so I sat about ten rows back and in the middle of the lecture theatre. As students entered the lecture theatre they sat in front, behind and beside me. Those sitting next to me nodded, however there was no attempt to communicate with me. I felt like an old dog in a litter of kittens, and very alone. The students were all so young. I had lost confidence in my ability to verbally communicate and I believed, rightly or wrongly, that I had nothing in common with my fellow students. I was isolated by my age, language difficulties and low self-esteem. I understood very little of what M. Ludwig said; I even had difficulty understanding notes he wrote on the whiteboard.

My isolation was situational. I had a close family and plenty of good friends but in the university environment, I was very isolated. As I sat in the auditorium I was apprehensive and wondered how I would cope in this foreign learning environment. I felt alone, and knew there was nothing I could do about it. I certainly wasn't prepared to impose myself on the young people around me, who I knew wouldn't want anything to do with someone old enough to be their grandfather.

I had studied French subjects part-time at Sydney University, off and on, for four years. I studied Political French Cinema. The final examination required pairs of students to give a presentation on a particular film. I sat in this class of young people for half the semester and wondered what planet these kids lived on. It wasn't any planet I knew existed. The course dealt with films in a social context so the students necessarily had to express their individual social attitudes. Their attitudes and opinions were so completely different from mine that, as much as possible, I kept quiet in class. I didn't acknowledge anyone, nor did anyone acknowledge me, before, after or during class. There were fifteen students in the tutorial and there could only be seven pairs of students. We were given a choice of films, and had to nominate which film we wanted to present. I noticed two young women who were obviously good friends sitting together. They were asked first, in turn, which film they wanted to present. They each nominated Loriet's *Welcome*. It was soon my turn so I nominated *Welcome*. I surmised that I would be a third person, with everyone else in pairs, so I would give a solo presentation. I deliberately isolated myself because I didn't think any student would want to give a presentation with me.

A week later at the end of the tutorial, one of the girls who had chosen *Welcome* approached me.

"Hi Russell, my name's Maria. Maggie and I want to get started on the presentation, so can we get together soon?"

I was very surprised.

"Sure, when and where will we meet?"

"Give me your phone number and email address and I will talk to Maggie."

Maria and Maggie just assumed that I was to be part of the presentation. It never occurred to me that two young women, who were friends, would want to include me, an elderly man in their presentation.

We met every Thursday at midday for the next seven weeks before we had to give the presentation. We had to decide how we were to present the film, about a young refugee who came to Calais with the intention of escaping France to settle in England. It raised issues of how refugees were treated in France. I suggested that we have a debate with one person the moderator, one person to argue the case for taking a hardline approach to asylum seekers and the other person to argue in favour of a sympathetic approach.

The girls decided I would be the bad guy and take the position of Marie La Penn (the leader of the extreme right-wing political party). Maria was the moderator and Maggie took the sympathetic view.

It would be difficult to imagine three people with less in common. Maria was early twenties and Japanese, Maggie was early thirties and Mauritian and I was an elderly Anglo Saxon. The cultural differences, ages and characters—Maria was gentle, shy and subtly got what she wanted, Maggie was gregarious and held strong views and I was used to telling people what to do, having spent my life in management positions. Our life experiences were totally different. The two young women were clever students, far smarter and more knowledgeable than me. Maggie's level of French was very advanced. During our discussions from time to time our different cultures and attitudes revealed themselves, not in any way as conflict but as points of view. The fact was, our differences were our strengths.

I looked forward to our regular meetings. Maggie formed a group of three on Facebook and we regularly communicated. There was no discussion about our personal lives, our private likes or dislikes; the common goal was restricted to giving a first-class presentation. We all received distinctions for the course. More importantly, it ended my isolation. I didn't end it; in fact, my intention had been to further isolate myself even though it was the last thing I really wanted. Maria and Maggie ended my isolation. I was my own worst enemy. I needed to divorce myself from my inferiority complex, fear of rejection, or whatever was driving me and participate in the exercise. If I wanted to initially do a presentation with Maria and Maggie, and decided they didn't want to give a presentation with me, I should have been able to accept the rejection, and move on. It took years of psychiatric treatment before I was able to accept that nothing was personal.

As I sat in the lecture theatre trying to understand M. Ludwig, I wondered if there were Marias and Maggies at the Sorbonne but I subconsciously realised I must accept personal responsibility for any isolation I felt. I very much doubted that I would be lucky enough to meet another Maria and Maggie.

The other form of isolation was created by language. This was why some, not all, migrants that came to Australia formed enclaves. They needed to be close to persons with whom they had a cultural and language affinity to enable them to have the social interaction and feeling of community everyone needs. It was only natural.

My limited understanding was not caused by lack of trying to assimilate in Paris. I spent considerable time in restaurants and bars. I frequented the bar closest to where I lived in the mornings, before Farid opened. Each day I visited Farid, but at various times depending on what else I was doing. As was my practice in Cronulla, I always read the newspaper.

After my disappointing first day at the Sorbonne, I determined to learn the language in order to avoid isolation. I purchased *Le Monde* newspaper, but I found this far too difficult so I read *Le Parisien*. Initially I could read less than half the stories, however I used a dictionary so my vocabulary improved fairly quickly. Language was also situational. Within four weeks I developed a reasonable vocabulary for news, however I was virtually illiterate when it came to fashion or the arts.

In the ten years before I went to the Sorbonne I, from time to time, undertook courses in French at Alliance Francaise in Sydney. I spent months in group classes that achieved very little. They were dominated by a few people who had a superior knowledge of French, and there was no academic rigour, no process where individual progress could be monitored. They were fun, but I found it difficult to progress my French language skills in that environment. I considered enrolling at Alliance Francaise in Paris, but dismissed it. In hindsight this was a huge mistake; if I had enrolled in Alliance Francaise, I would have acquired French language skills quickly. I didn't realise it at the time but Alliance Francaise had specialist courses for international students. I was too dumb to enquire, at my great cost.

One challenge I found almost impossible to overcome was to develop everyday conversation. I was able to have limited conversation at Farid's bar, however at other places it was difficult. I couldn't talk to barmen, including Farid, because they were too busy and I was too shy to strike up a conversation with strangers. I did, however, develop a technique to have at least some conversation. I took a few words from *Le Parisien* that I was reading, and asked a stranger what it meant. I did this quite often and every single time I asked a stranger to explain something, there was always a cheerful willingness to help me. This helped me improve my French as I then asked a few follow-up questions. I was careful not to push the boundaries of French kindness too far.

As I walked and cycled the streets of Paris I become acutely aware of middle-aged men, and some women too, sitting on the footpaths. One hundred metres from my apartment a middle-aged man sat day in, day out on the footpath. On the opposite side of the street a woman had marked her place outside the local patisserie. There were about six other men and women in similar situations near my home. They were obviously poor; their clothes were dilapidated and drab. They sat on the footpath day after day, a begging bowl in front of them, with seemingly nothing to do.

I decided that this was an opportunity for me to learn to speak French. I sat on the footpath beside a homeless man. I was sure he would enjoy the company of a stranger to break the monotony of his day. I prepared for the occasion by wearing my oldest pair of jeans and a crumpled old shirt. I had never been accused of having any regard for sartorial elegance and it was far easier for me to merge within a homeless environment than a businessman's black-tie dinner party. As I sat beside him, he gave me a toothless smile. I returned the smile with my gappy teeth.

"Bonjour," I said.

"Bonjour," he replied

I asked how he was and he said he was ok. I had a great deal of difficulty communicating with him and there was only a smattering of words that we seemed to have in common. Later, I sat beside the woman outside the patisserie. She immediately rose to her feet and walked away. I concluded that I was not attractive to middle-aged homeless women. Over the next week I sat next to a number of homeless men. Some men didn't seem to understand me at all; with others, the conversation was extremely basic.

Three nights a week I discussed various issues with Damien, always in English. One particular night he cooked veal cutlets with vegetables. We sat down, and started to eat.

"I am very disappointed that I can't speak French with anyone. I sit beside the homeless men around the corner, and try to speak to them but I just can't communicate. It must be my accent. I'm really frustrated."

Damien wiped his mouth with his napkin. "Those men are Bulgarian," he said. "They cannot speak French."

Damien thought it was funny, I didn't. Sometimes I had tunnel vision and followed my instincts rather than exercised common sense. Enrolling in Alliance Francaise or engaging with lawyers or other professionals were obvious ways to improve my speaking skills. I took the easy way out by attempting to speak to seemingly homeless people with nothing better to do than to speak to me. Maybe I wasn't taking the easy way out. The study of philosophy relates to questions of our existence, our being, who we are. My single unit study of Reality, Ethics and Art, at Sydney University, had already awakened my senses to the choices I made, how I made those choices, and what the ethical framework was within which I existed. My choices reflected coming home. My roots were in southern England where The Hodge was the village idiot. My family were marginal farmers in Hill End. That's where I came from, that's where, in Paris, I went back to.

Seven

Port de Clingancourt was totally different to Saint Michel. Saint Michel was near the centre of Paris, with wide boulevards, quaint old-style buildings, and narrow laneways that typified an inner city. The Metro at Port de Clingancourt exited onto a huge roundabout. I was very fortunate when I arrived that I chose the nearest exit to the university. The roundabout was so wide it didn't appear to be a roundabout. A combination of wide boulevards and narrow rues spewed out of the circular road. Standing where I exited the Metro, I could see large trees, swathes of traffic, and seemingly distant high-rise buildings on the road on the far side of the roundabout. Across the road were other Metro exits and various eating establishments, fast food outlets, bus parking stations.

The unexpected change from St. Michel to Port Clingancourt meant I had to establish routines that anchored myself to the area. My life was one of attachment and habit. Attaching myself to places and people I felt comfortable with enabled me to function effectively. There was no library or place to study at the university. The library was situated in a different part of Port Clingancourt.

Within days of lectures starting I went to the University Library at Port de Clingancourt. I walked back to the Metro exit, crossed the road, walked past McDonalds, and turned into a small rue, Rue Letort. It was a one-way street that had cars parked on either side with barely enough space for a car to transit. At the start of the rue was a Velib station. I walked down the footpath on the left-hand side. The footpath was very narrow. I could step from one side of the footpath to the other. It was littered with rubbish and I could see large garbage receptacles in the distance.

The first person I noticed was a young woman sitting on the footpath thirty metres from the start of Rue Letort. She was very large, wore a chocolate-coloured dress and a long-sleeved grey blouse and a shawl. She was breastfeeding. A pram was nearby. The pram was so dilapidated that it appeared incapable of being pushed. I couldn't avoid the woman as she took up most of the footpath and I had to move to the edge in order to pass.

Every day for a week, I said "bonjour" and she was always feeding the baby. I never saw her in the afternoon when I returned from the library. Every day she sat on the footpath feeding her baby, with a plastic cup in front of her. A plastic cup was a tool of the trade for people begging on the street. The other tool of the trade was either a dog or a baby. A dog or a baby provides a marketing edge. Some days I put money in her plastic cup—one or two euros.

Some days I just said, "Bonjour."

She always responded with "Bonjour."

I never saw the child as she was always suckling. One day I noticed the mother was distracted and the child, wearing a nappy, was on the edge of the footpath where a car was reversing into an empty space. I took the child by the hand and walked her slowly back to her mother. The toddler's clothes were drab and not particularly clean. Her mother grabbed the toddler by the hand, and with an expressionless face turned away from me and deposited the child in the nearby pram. I was irrationally miffed by her lack of gratitude. I grabbed the toddler because I sensed she was in danger, not because I wanted thanks.

I needed a comfortable place to eat between the university and the library. Within twenty metres of the exit was the Royal Clingancourt Bar Brasserie. It was the closest and most obvious place for me to patronise. It had a long and fairly narrow eating area. There was no other place to eat unless I crossed the road. I noticed a restaurant bar across the road and in fact I passed it to go to the library but it didn't appeal to me. It was very typical in size, décor and layout of many Parisian bar restaurants and was very similar to the Royal Clingancourt Bar Brasserie. I preferred to drink coffee and eat simple food in places that were a bit different. I tried to avoid restaurants that relied on turnover to make a profit and preferred personal attention to quick cheap service. I didn't like patronising this bar/restaurant but it seemed the best of a bad lot.

After ten days of eating and having coffee at the Royal, I found it impersonal and cold. One day, for no apparent reason, returning from the library, I decided not to enter the Royal. I veered to the right and noticed a small lane called Passage de Mont Cenis. As I entered the passage I noticed a couple of tables on the footpath outside a doorway.

It was three o'clock in the afternoon. I walked inside the restaurant and glanced at the interior. Other than it being small, I didn't specifically observe its interior as I was immediately attracted to its size with its potential for intimacy. I approached the man at the bar. He was a large man of Arabic appearance, casually dressed and leaning against the wall polishing a glass.

"Can I use the toilet please?" I asked.

He stared at me and started shouting. I didn't know what he was saying; he was speaking very quickly in French. I heard the word "jamais" which I knew meant never.

I understood using the toilet was not an option so I changed the subject. "I would like to eat please?"

He resumed shouting and I didn't understand what he said but I heard the word "McDonalds".

I had the impression that I wasn't allowed to use his toilet, and if I wanted to eat then I should go across the road to McDonalds. I was taken aback by the aggression in his voice. His jaw was firmly set, his lips were drawn tight, and he leant towards me with a scowl. My reaction was instinctive and immediate.

"Vous êtes très gentile monsieur," I calmly said as I retreated from his nastiness. The sarcasm was lost on him. I resolved never to return. It was a shame because it was the quaint type of restaurant I liked to patronise. As I sat in my room that night I was perplexed and wondered why I had behaved in such an uncharacteristic way. If I was in Australia, I would have told him to stick his restaurant up his arse. I was never one to avoid confrontation—to the contrary, I thrived on it.

Descartes determined there was a division between the mind and the body and that wisdom came from the application of the mind independently of emotion. He hypothesised that our thinking related to what was the right thing to do, whereas perhaps the question was what was the wise thing to do? Wisdom didn't come from our emotions. Our emotions were embedded in our attitudes, life experiences, self-esteem and our environment. These emotions were reactive and irrational.

My response to Fahat, the rude restaurant owner, was not intellectual, nor was it because I thought it was the right way to react. If wisdom derived from thinking, and I was not thinking, ipso facto, my response could only have been emotional. My emotional response at this time was environmental. I had settled well into the Sorbonne, I had secure accommodation and a fitness regime that provided recreational activity. I was settled emotionally and I was content, despite issues with Damien. While I had issues with language, isolation and understanding lecturers, the experience was still novel and exciting so I didn't feel any pressure. While my reaction to Fahat was emotional, if I considered the situation intellectually, I would have reacted the same way, so my reaction was at once emotional and wise. Sadly, the convergence of emotion and wisdom soon disappeared.

Eight

From the moment I met Romain he showed an interest in helping me assimilate into French society. I needed a badminton racquet, so Romain offered to take me to the store in Chatalet.

Chatelet was near the river Seine. As it wound through the centre of Paris the Seine was a concrete canal, a very beautiful canal but concrete all the same. Many bridges crossed it. Romain showed me the Pont D'Arcole which crossed the Seine where the river was quite wide. The Hotel Ville, close to the pont, resembled a palace; a huge building with turrets, ornate carvings, windows curved at the top, it was a magnificent structure. We walked past the hotel and within five minutes were in Rue des Lombards, a long narrow street, accessible only by pedestrians. Rue des Lombards intersected with similar rues. It was only in Paris where there were wide busy boulevards that oases of pedestrian walkways filled with pedestrians and all manner and types of eateries existed. Romain and I entered the Yonex shop, and Romain stood behind me like a watchful mother. I chose a suitable badminton racquet and had little difficulty negotiating the purchase. Being with Romain and chatting about Paris while we walked, and then buying the racquet were important but small steps to increasing my confidence, and peace of mind, in Paris.

I chose badminton as an optional subject because it had no academic content. I also knew that it wouldn't be demanding. I was a reasonably accomplished tennis player, in my own eyes at least, and had played squash when I was younger. I regarded badminton as a fancy form of shuttlecock. Shuttlecock was a simple game involving two players with bats hitting a cork with feathers attached. In Australia, families commonly played shuttlecock on outings to the beach or on picnics in the national parks.

The badminton courts were fairly close to the gymnasium. I packed my gym bag so that I could have a workout after my badminton session. I alighted at Port Royale and walked down a narrow footpath to the indoor courts. I walked down a wide flight of stairs, found the change rooms and changed into my badminton gear. I must admit I looked the part. I wore a very nice pair of freshly ironed grey shorts, a white T-shirt, brand-new gym shoes and carried a swish badminton racquet.

I walked through some swing doors and onto the courts. I was amazed by the size of the courts. I didn't imagine that there would be nine full-size badminton courts. I was the first to arrive and soon students started to trickle onto the courts.

The first student walked towards me and said, "Bonjour, Professeur."

I replied, "Bonjour! But I am not the teacher, I am a student."

I was accustomed to the looks of disbelief that followed my declaration that I was a student. A few other students similarly mistook me for the teacher. The actual teacher arrived just before the appointed time. He was very fit-looking, about forty years of age. If he had hair, we would be mistaken for twins. The students' mistake was very understandable.

The obligatory marking of the role took place and the class started. Le Prof required us to run around the gym. Along with the thirty-five other students in the class, I started to run around the outside edge of the gym. Le Prof was never satisfied with the level of effort. As various students dropped the pace they were named and shamed. I was no exception; in fact, I seemed to be singled out. Even I understood "Vieillard plus vite" (faster, old man). At the point where my lungs were bursting Le Prof stopped the run. I doubled over and put my hands on my knees. I couldn't blow out a candle.

I glanced sideways and noticed a young woman jogging on the spot, breathing normally. There wasn't a bead of sweat in sight. I stood up, straightened, stretched my back, and returned her friendly smile. She was medium height with shiny long brown hair and dark eyes. A cute little upturned nose punctuated her face. Stomach rolls spewed over, and bulging thighs stretched, her tight lycra slacks. Large flabby arms and a couple of chins protruded from the extremities of her loose-fitting T-shirt. As I tried to breathe normally another student greeted her. I then knew that her name was Sabine.

Le Prof didn't let us cool down. The shuttlecock that I played with as a child was a *ballon* at the Sorbonne. We used it for skill training. We were split into pairs. My partner was a fit young man who approached me, and asked me if we could practise together. I lay on my back, threw up the *ballon*, and caught it when it fell at the same time as my partner hit another one over the back of my head, which I then hit before jumping to my feet. I hated four-count squats. Le Prof gave us the equivalent of four-count squats incorporating hand/eye co-ordination skills.

We played a series of singles matches. This was the first time I had played badminton. I was a chronic over-achiever so naturally I considered that I was one of the better players in the group, particularly as half the group were women. I didn't realise that the object of the matches was to determine our ranking in the group. I faced the immediate difficulty that I couldn't understand instructions in French. I didn't have any French vocabulary relating to sport, yet I wanted to be immersed in the French language. I told everyone I didn't want to speak English.

The mix of young men and women was about equal. Some men and women were very good exponents of the game, other players had little ability. The males were very competitive and hated being beaten by an old man. Some women were very competitive but in the main winning or losing against me didn't matter much. The badminton game was very valuable in learning communication skills. It was a different environment than classes. In classes I sat, benignly listening and whether or not I understood made no difference to anyone else. I was the only one affected. With badminton, I was given instructions regarding who to play with, what format practice was to take, what skills I was to practise, and how to play and record matches. I didn't understand what I was supposed to do, and there was much confusion. Students spoke to me in French, moved me by the arm and used sign language to tell me what to do. If this was very frustrating for other students they never showed it.

During the course of the grading matches Le Prof announced that I must play Sabine. Sabine walked towards court five and the whole group surrounded the court. I guessed that he suspended all other games to make my match with Sabine a feature event. I was most unhappy with this turn of events. I felt it was unfair to Sabine and I didn't want to embarrass her. I knew she was awkward and not mobile and I perceived I would be able to run her round the court and beat her comfortably.

Perceptions were interesting. We are bombarded and overwhelmed with advertising, news reports and commentary, all of which cause us to develop perceptions, attitudes and prejudices. The first lesson in high school economics was that it was not logical to take a specific example from which to generalise. If John was an idiot it didn't follow that all Johns were idiots. The reverse, false logic arose from stereotyping. The assumption that a specific follows from the general. Fat people were lazy and unfit, thin people were energetic, groups of Arabic young men were to be feared, boat people took our jobs, the unemployed were dole bludgers. The media bombardment clouded our vision, created stereotypes and inhibited our ability to see nuances so as to assess differences. My perception of Sabine, based on her physical appearance, was she was unfit, uncoordinated and a poor athlete. My perception didn't allow me to cognitively process the simple fact that, minutes earlier, she easily completed a grueling aerobic session.

I decided that I would let Sabine win a few points. The winner was the first person to win eleven points, but there must be a margin of two points. If there was not a two-point margin when a player reached eleven points, the game continued until one player led by two points. I didn't expect the game to be extended.

Sabine served first. I took it easy and the score was 4–1 in Sabine's favour. After my serve the score was 7–3 in Sabine's favour. OK, I would now move in for the kill. She had scored enough points not to be embarrassed by losing. I was very tactical and knew how to beat her. I would hit the *ballon* to the back of the court and then when she returned the *ballon* I would drop it short. I assumed she had neither the speed nor the agility to reach the *ballon* from the back of the court.

Sabine served. Four points later Sabine won 11–3. There was noisy and joyous acclaim from the onlookers. I thought that Sabine's yell as she jumped high in the air, her hands above her head, a touch unnecessary. It wasn't a Toyota ad! As I shook Sabine's hand I felt embarrassed and a bit humiliated by my failure. Any thoughts that I may have had some ability as a badminton player vanished. Except against novice players, I tried hard to win and enjoyed playing the games without expectations of success or failure.

Playing for fun, for the sake of the sport itself, was a seismic shift in my attitude. All my life I lived for sport. I was still playing rugby union in my thirties, and was a very keen tennis player. I hated losing. No matter how far I was behind I never gave up. I suspect that badminton represented my life at the time. I was at the Sorbonne, any hope of achieving decent results had already evaporated, so I was in survival mode. I soon realised badminton was no different—I was never going to be very good, all I could do was to survive. Strangely, I accepted, in badminton, the concept of enjoying the journey and ignoring the results. It's a pity that it didn't translate into my academic studies.

Nine

The tutor for my first tutorial in the History of the Philosophy of Science was M. Kammerer. I was immediately struck by his youth. He appeared to be in his mid to late twenties. He seemed quite sporty with the type of flat stomach that quickly disappeared as men aged. He was very business-like. The tutorial, like all other tutorials at the Sorbonne, had over thirty students and lasted one and a half hours. M. Kammerer set the ground rules very quickly. He marked the roll and told students that attendance was compulsory and he expected them to keep up to date with their studies.

The tutorial passed without incident except that I understood very little of what he said. He spoke French very quickly and there was no consideration or compromise for anyone who might have language or understanding difficulties. I knew that after he asked a student a question, he marked their name off the role so he knew who had been asked questions.

The tutorials had a fixed routine. M. Kammerer, after marking the roll, spent half an hour asking questions. I found this part of the tutorial very stressful. I knew that sooner or later he would ask me a question. Even if I understood the question I doubted that I would have an adequate answer. Paradoxically I was not particularly worried about displaying my ignorance as my fellow students already knew my French language skills were poor. It was the uncertainty of when I would be asked the question that was stressful. The remaining hour, M. Kammerer lectured. He demanded absolute silence while he spoke. In one tutorial two students were speaking while he lectured and M. Kammerer told them to leave and said he would mark them absent from the tutorial. This was a significant penalty as the work in tutorials and the tutorial exams counted for fifty percent of the final mark.

In the first tutorial (the Sorbonne calls a tutorial a TD) I asked M. Kammerer to speak more slowly. He looked at me sympathetically, carefully weighed up my request and said "Non".

I was somewhat intrigued by Kammerer's approach to teaching, particularly in a university environment. I always understood a university was a place where there was freedom of thought and expression and pass or failure was a personal responsibility. I had studied in two universities for a total of ten years and had never seen students ejected from a tutorial or lecture even in cases where students were quite disruptive. The question it raised was, what was the best environment in which students learn? M. Kammerer created an environment based on coercion. It was successful—however, there were alternative means of keeping students' attention and enabling them to learn. I had been a high school teacher. I didn't have the personality to teach like M. Kammerer. I didn't have the skills to take control of a class and exercise brute power. I had to find another way.

***

I started teaching at Ashfield Boys High School when I was twenty years of age. I taught Year Twelve economics and geography and a couple of young men in the class were older than me. The school had a large, mainly Greek, migrant population. The school was ruled with an iron rod as behaviour problems and truancy were rife. Every student at the school had their own card. It was marked into squares with the days of the week along the top of the card and the numbers one to eight on the left-hand side. Every lesson every student presented his card to the teacher who put a stamp in the square that corresponded to the day of the week and the period. The teaching day consisted of eight periods. In this way, the school knew exactly who was absent and at the end of the day the secretary checked every card to ensure that each student had attended every class. My stamp was C8.

In my first year of teaching I had to have an inspection so that I could obtain a teaching certificate. On one particular day, I had taught the first period when an inspector came into the staff room. I was introduced to Mr. Simpson who advised me that he was here to see me teach and he had to leave by lunchtime. I was not programmed to teach that morning.

After I was introduced he said, "Are you related to THE Russell Hodge?"

"He was my grandfather."

"He was the most famous headmaster in the department," Simpson said. "He was brilliant. You would be the great nephew of Harry Hodge, the headmaster at Raymond Terrace. I knew your grandfather and Harry very well."

"I suppose you know my Uncle Brian," I remarked somewhat ironically.

"Of course I do! He is teaching at Sydney Tech High."

I came from a long line of teachers. My grandmother, grandfather, great uncle, my father's three brothers and their wives were all schoolteachers employed by the New South Wales Department of Education.

After consultation between Jack Tilburn my subject master and Mr. Simpson, Jack Tilburn told me I must give a lesson to a Year Eleven geography class. I was aghast. Not only had I not prepared a lesson, but this was a particularly challenging class filled with difficult disrespectful teenage boys. I protested.

Mr. Simpson said, "You'll be 'right! Teaching is in your blood."

I knew there would be blood and it would be mine!

I had until recess to prepare a lesson. I was familiar with the syllabus because I was teaching another Year Eleven geography class. It was a class of interested, intelligent students. Jack Tilburn told me to teach the formation of a glacier.

I pondered how to teach this class. Their regular teacher had about four years of experience. He was a rough, tough teacher with no tolerance for insolence or disruptive behaviour. The boys were afraid to cross him; his discipline was strict and effective. I weighed fifty-four kilos and was one hundred and sixty-three centimetres tall. Rough and tough I was not.

I walked into the classroom. There was initial silence as the boys expected their regular teacher. I addressed them.

"Hello boys. I am teaching you today." There was a low rumble. As the boys digested this statement, I continued. "Mr. Simpson, an inspector from the education department, will come into the class in a few minutes. He will tell you that he is here to see how well you are learning and how you are behaving. He will tell you that you boys are on trial. This is not true. He is really here to see how well I can teach. If I pass the inspection, I can keep teaching. If I fail, I will be pulling beers at the local pub. What I want you to do is to keep your mouths shut, answer my questions and be interested and enthusiastic."

There was a great deal of mirth. At least the boys are happy, I thought to myself.

"You can't pull beers sir, you can't see over the bar," Paul Pinkewich called out.

I knew Pinkewich. He was rarely at school. He was a cheeky, irrepressible young man who was a champion table tennis player. His absences were due to his table tennis tournament commitments.

Before I could respond the door opened and in walked Mr. Simpson. There was immediate silence.

"Good morning boys," he said. "I am Mr. Simpson. I'm an inspector from the education department. I am here to see how well you are learning and how you behave in class. I am watching you. Carry on Mr. Hodge."

I stood at the front of the class and leant against the table. I was struck by an eerie feeling of being watched by twenty-five silent boys. For the first time, I could hear the rumble of traffic on the very busy Liverpool Road, ten metres from the classroom.

I commenced. "Today we are going skiing in the Snowy Mountains."

"You can't ski, sir," Pinkewich called out.

I heard a low hiss from the other boys. All the boys near him turned to look at him. The boy next to him closed his fist and shook it under the table. I saw a look of fear cross Pinkewich's face.

"You're right, Pinkewich. Next time put your hand up."

"Sorry, sir."

I proceeded to ask a series of questions, such as, "Who has been to the Snowy Mountains? Does the snow melt? What happens if the snow doesn't melt? Does the snow compact? What effect does compacting snow have on the land underneath?" I asked for volunteers to draw a glacial valley on the blackboard. The boys nominated a student with an artistic bent who happily obliged.

I had difficulty teaching. Every time I asked a question there was a plethora of hands of boys demanding I ask them to answer the question. Nobody spoke out of turn. The boys appeared interested and engaged. The silence, interest and apparent enthusiasm were totally foreign to me.

Suddenly Mr. Simpson got up from the back of the class, walked towards the door and said to the boys, "You have done well." He left the room and closed the door behind him.

There was silence. I sat on the edge of the table, my legs dangling.

"Two schooners of new and a vodka and orange please sir," Pinkewich called out.

There was uproarious laughter, even I thought it was funny. I eventually settled the class down and they seemed to want me to continue the lesson, which I did.

Mr. Simpson described me as a gifted teacher, who was able to keep the class interested and engaged. He recommended that I be issued with a teaching certificate.

Teenage boys are no different from any one else. I was honest and respectful to the boys in the class, and they responded as I expected they would.

In a way, M. Kammerer educated me. As a student, and an educator, I thought good teaching was about engaging students and presenting material in an interesting way. Only incompetent, personality-deficient teachers resorted to bullying and autocratic control; M. Kammerer fitted the profile. As the semester advanced, I came to regard M. Kammerer as an excellent teacher. Sure, the environment was coercive, but his objective was to help students pass the subject. He forced everyone firstly to turn up, and secondly come prepared or be embarrassed, marked down by an inability to answer his questions. It's not the way that I taught, not the way I liked to be taught, but it was an effective method by a caring tutor.

Ten

I quickly established myself, settled into lectures and tutorials, found the library and developed a daily routine. Two weeks after lectures started, I received an early morning phone call from a friend holidaying in the Maldives. He was ringing to tell me that my good friend Greg was in hospital and would probably die.

I knew that Greg and Mandy were in the Maldives with a group of friends from the Sutherland Shire. The phone call was long and painful but I wanted to know every detail, not from a sense of morbid voyeurism but to absorb and understand the sequence of events. As the phone call continued my imagination drifted in and out of the setting and the events.

The group had chartered a luxury cruiser to take six couples off the coast to find the best surf. Umbrellas were anchored to the deck of the cruiser. The cruiser motored to a reef somewhere off the coast of the Maldives. The women lounged in the sun, sharing stories of their children and grandchildren while the men surfed. Jet skis took the men and their surfboards to the perfect swell. There were a couple of jet skis manned by the crew.

Greg and his surfing mates, aged in their late fifties and early sixties, considered paddling for a wave was passé. Their preferred method was to ride in a tender to the break, surf the break and then have the tender pick them up and transport them back to the break.

Mandy was a keen photographer who decided to watch Greg surf and take photos. Mandy jumped onto the back of a tender and zoomed towards the reef. She couldn't get close, as the swell was too large. She screwed the telescopic lens to her camera, and saw Greg through the lens sitting on his board, with his arm in the air and then slump onto his board. She knew he was in trouble. She grabbed her driver and urgently told him to get him but they were too far away. He radioed the other tender driver who picked Greg up and took him to the cruiser.

Greg was barely conscious. It took six men to pull Greg up onto the deck. Greg lay on the deck, incoherent, semi-conscious and violently vomiting. The skipper of the cruiser radioed the mainland for urgent assistance. The Maldives was a Muslim country and it was the hour of prayers—there was no response. As the cruiser was a long way from the mainland they had to wait for the speedboat to arrive to take Greg to hospital.

The speedboat arrived and the crew lowered Greg onto its deck. Greg was obviously very ill. Abdul, the tour agent, was waiting beside his motorcycle for Greg when he reached the mainland. He helped load Greg into an ambulance and Mandy rode with him. For Mandy, Greg's trip to the hospital in the ambulance was a blur. Mandy was in the ambulance, siren blaring, stopping and accelerating, swerving through narrow streets. Abdul was ahead on the bike, clearing the way for the ambulance. Greg was admitted to hospital and given an urgent CT scan. After the scan, the doctor sat beside Mandy in the waiting room.

"Your husband has massive bleeding in the lining of his brain," the doctor said. "You should prepare yourself for the fact he is going to die. Your only hope is an operation at the main hospital."

Greg was discharged from the hospital before he was rushed to the main hospital by ambulance. There was only one neurosurgeon in the Maldives. There were many islands on the Maldives with hospitals needing a neurosurgeon, and he could be anywhere. Luckily, he was at the main hospital. Greg was admitted into casualty, and Mandy spoke to the neurosurgeon. Later, Mandy described him to me as a tall man. She said he wore a sarong, a polo-neck shirt and thongs covered his feet. There was little time to speak. The doctor told Mandy that Greg had less than two hours to live if he didn't operate.

Mandy understood that Greg's injury was so severe that in normal circumstances the surgeon would refuse to operate. One of Greg's pupils had blown out, a sure sign of imminent death.

Mandy saw the surgeon leave the operating theatre. He had blood on his shoes from the blood that spurted out of the lining in Greg's brain where a hole had been bored. He gave the thumbs up to Mandy. Greg had survived the operation and was now in intensive care.

The public hospital was huge. Mandy was in shock. She wasn't able to absorb the difference in culture between the Maldives and her own Western society. She was vaguely aware of full burkhas, hijabs, sarongs and sandals as she sat by Greg in intensive care. The difference between the main wards and intensive care was a red line drawn on the floor and a curtain shielding patients from public view.

Some hours after Greg was placed in intensive care, Mandy met the neurosurgeon.

"Your husband survived the operation," he said.

"What did you do?"

"I bored a hole in his head to drain the blood from his brain."

"Will he be alright?"

"I don't know. All we can do is wait."

The words in crude form seemed unhelpful. The tone was empathetic. It was the Muslim way of saying it was in the hands of Allah.

"Do we know if the operation was successful?" Mandy asked.

"No. He is too sick to move. I cannot give him a CT scan to find out and even if I could operate I don't have the equipment. We have to wait."

Mandy and a friend met in a quiet place adjacent to the hospital. They sat together in sad silence. Mandy handed him Greg's phone. "You'd better ring Russell."

My studies at the Sorbonne no longer had any point or purpose. I was sick with worry and I couldn't concentrate. Of course, I went through the motions. I had established a routine of breakfast, lectures, gym and study depending on the day of the week. I continued my almost daily walk to the library. Mechanically walking down the narrow rue, my mind was a blank. I was miserable and alone. Perhaps I subconsciously better understood the value of humanity and the importance of life, which is why I stopped to speak to the woman with the toddler.

I asked her what she would like. She said "manger". I nodded my head and I followed her across the road to KFC. She left the pram on the footpath and carried the toddler. She had a huge smile on her face. We approached the counter.

The young girl refused to serve us and said she would get the manager. The manager asked if she had money. I told him I was paying and that I had plenty of money. She ordered twenty-two euros of food, enough to feed a family.

Later that night I recounted this to Damien. He said there was a law in France that everyone had a right to be served. A shopkeeper could only refuse to serve someone if they didn't have money to pay for what they wanted.

Days passed and Greg's life still hung in the balance. I rang Mandy.

"How's Greg, is he going to be all right, are you ok?" the words tumbled out in a confused rush of multiple questions.

"I'm good, but I don't know what's going to happen to Greg. I saw the neurosurgeon this morning. His English is pretty good but he's got this thick accent and talks technically so I had trouble understanding him. As far as I could gather Greg is in a critical condition and the doctor doesn't know if he will survive. He told me I had to decide whether to leave him here or move him to Singapore. Either way he might die. I didn't have a clue so I asked the surgeon what he would do if Greg were his child. He said he would move him, so that's what I'm going to do."

And so it passed. Greg remained in intensive care ready to be moved to Singapore. Over subsequent days I spoke to Mandy and each of their four boys.

I was in a petite rue at St. Michel, the Latin quarter of Paris. It was a small lane with magnificent tall buildings above a melange of restaurants. It was a beautiful autumn day, warm and no wind. I stood in a patch of sunlight surrounded by crowds of people, but I was alone and distressed. The tears streamed down my face. I was speaking to Greg's son, Jack. I had telephoned him to give him support. He was so positive and he told me his father was on a ferry. The medevac jet had landed on an adjacent island. I couldn't stop crying. I rang Jack to support and comfort him but I was the one in real distress, while he was so positive.

With Greg so sick, I was very frustrated with the coldness and impersonal service at the Royal. I felt alone, and needed some normality. Normality to me was small intimate eating places. I decided to again try the quaint establishment, where weeks before the barman had told me to go to McDonalds.

It was with trepidation that I entered the restaurant. My nemesis was nowhere to be seen when I entered, and except for one other person the restaurant was empty. I had time to look around. On the left as I walked in was a bain-marie that held various hot and cold foods. Behind these were cooking appliances and a tiled wall. The bar was on the right-hand side and took up most of the wall. I looked to the right and saw an enormous Alsatian dog asleep on the floor. There was only seating for about twelve people. The seating arrangements consisted of some comfortable chairs with a table between, a couch on the wall and ordinary table and chairs. The walls of the restaurant were decorated with colourful paintings. Various knick-knacks were attached to the wall. There was clearly an Arabic influence.

My nemesis appeared at the end of the bar. We exchanged *bonjours* and I asked him if he was open for lunch. He confirmed he was.

"When I came here two weeks ago you were very nasty," I said in broken French. "You would not let me use the toilet and you told me to go to McDonalds."

He didn't speak English at all. The ensuing conversation was a combination of French, repeating what was said, and gesticulation. I understood that when I came in his toilet was blocked. It had been blocked for ten days because of a problem in the street. He took me by the arm into the toilet so that I understood. He said he was sorry about how he spoke to me.

I ordered a meal. Bread, steak, chips and white coffee cost fourteen euros. The ambience was everything that I wanted in a restaurant. The food was very good and cheap. The restaurant satisfied my basic human needs. Bread, steak and chips were staples in my diet at home—well, not quite, Chris Penfold insisted chips on buttered bread were inconsistent with a healthy diet, so I had eliminated these from my diet. It was not difficult to discard Chris' sage advice given my diminishing emotional health. The small restaurant and simple staple food moved me into my comfort zone.

While I ate, I pictured Greg lying motionless in a Singapore hospital. He had an emergency operation. He had no cognition. He lay still with tubes inserted into him. He resembled a broken doll. Mandy and their four sons stood at his bedside. They held his hand, they talked to him. But for his soft breathing, Greg showed no sign of life.

Three weeks after Greg first slumped on his surfboard, he lay motionless in intensive care in a Singapore hospital, showing no signs of life. One of his sons decided to play his favourite song, *Ruby Tuesday*, on the iPhone they'd attached to speakers beside his bed. At first nothing happened. Then, about halfway into the song, Greg's lips began to quiver. At first the family didn't know what was happening. His eyes were still closed. It was Mandy who realised that Greg was singing along—silently of course—to the song. Then they noticed that he'd begun to tap his finger to the beat of the tune. Tears flowed. When they got home to Sydney, the whole family had 'Ruby Tuesday' tattooed on their upper arms.

My relief was palpable. I couldn't wait to ring Greg and my attitude to life and studies changed dramatically. I felt as if a dead weight was lifted from my shoulders. My walk to the library now had purpose. My interest in philosophy, my surroundings and activities was rejuvenated. I was no longer lost.

Eleven

It was three weeks before I approached Mme Renault, the lecturer in Philosophie Moderne. She lectured to over a hundred students, and often referred to texts. After the third lecture, I stood in line behind several students who wanted to know something or other. Finally, it was my turn.

"Can you tell me the texts you have referred to in the lecture please?" I asked.

"Look it up on the intranet." Her reply was dismissive as she looked over my shoulder towards the student standing behind me. I felt unimportant and rejected. I was taken aback, as it was unusual for me to be spoken to like this in Paris. My only real issue had been students and teachers pretending they didn't speak English. It never occurred to me that Mme Renault might have been very busy.

Mme Renault read from notes, in common with virtually every other lecturer, however from time to time she engaged the students. The lectures were given in a tiered theatre with students looking down on her. During the course of the lecture Mme Renault asked a general question. She identified a student volunteer, and when the student answered, invariably followed up with a discussion with that student. Only the students surrounding the chosen one heard the exchange. General noise and chattering permeated the theatre until Mme Renault resumed reading from her notes. It didn't matter to me, I couldn't understand her anyway.

Mme Renault's departure from the set routine of reading and her involvement of students was pedagogically admirable, the delivery less admirable. As a young teacher, I had attempted to do something similar at a religious private school.

Oatley Park was empty, well almost empty—I was there, spruiking. Saturday morning, and the nearby village was filled with shoppers, mostly mothers and children. I wondered if they could hear me? As far as I could tell, no one was listening. I watched the ebb and flow of the local population, stopping to chat, languidly leaning against telegraph poles, grabbing their children, rushing to an appointment, leisurely shopping—but I was unheard, invisible. I was perched on top of my stepladder very close to the iconic Oatley clock, a tribute to James Oatley, a watchmaker transported to the colonies, and pardoned by Governor Macquarie for his work as a clockmaker in the infant colony. My position adjacent to the Oatley Town Clock was symbolically appropriate. James Oatley was a sinner who gained redemption when pardoned by Governor Macquarie. I was not Governor Macquarie, but I brought redemption through the Lord with my stepladder, bible and megaphone.

I was twenty years old, teaching at Ashfield Boys High School, a fervent member of the Oatley Church of England, an evangelical church as far removed from the high Church of England as a Catholic priest was from sex with an adult. I lived the life of a Christian; no sex before marriage—sex was only available within marriage for procreation, and no alcohol—the elixir of the devil.

I had joined the youth fellowship of the church to be with my friends. Each week we sang hymns and churchy songs to catchy pop tunes. It was the music, the intoxication of group singing, that led me, who couldn't hold a note, to the Lord. The weekly fellowship singing sessions, led by Stewart, the curate who replaced the previous curate who hurriedly left at the same time as his girlfriend developed a bump in the lower stomach region, inspired my conversion to Christianity. Something about the words, the combined power of a group of people singing (to call it a choir was to dishonour the word) impacted my consciousness, common sense and rationality to the point where I believed a virgin could conceive.

Bible studies with the church elders and widows was one of my favourite activities. Followers of the Navigators movement such as myself lived their lives through strict adherence to the scriptures. My father, an atheist, had a natural instinct to live by the Word of God. Ephesians 5:22 was his favourite; wives must obey their husbands. These were not idle words—every day before my father went to work my mother polished his shoes. I brought the Word of the Lord into our household as I beseeched my siblings to repent, and in turn my father put the fear of the God into me—with a steel poker if I mentioned the words Jesus, God, prayer, Bible or any other word that could be remotely connected to Christianity. A compromise, as always, was reached. I only talked about my beliefs when he was too pissed to know what I was saying, which was most of the time he was home.

My father fought in World War II, on the frontline in Palestine in a flash spotter's unit, and when he was repatriated to Australia he joined the Air Force to later fly over Germany as a navigator in Lancaster bombers. He suffered from severe traumatic stress syndrome which he medicated with alcohol. I was a classic example of intergenerational traumatic stress syndrome transfer.

After two years teaching at Ashfield Boys High School, I informed my father that I had resigned from the Department of Education, and had been admitted to the Australian National University and Sydney University law schools. He was apoplectic with rage; he would have been less angry if I had shot my mother.

"You are stupid! You have a career, a steady job, no worries. Why would you want to leave it?"

"Your brothers are schoolteachers and they don't have a bob to their name. Mum doesn't work, we have a weekender, and you never whinge about money. I'm not going to be poor for the rest of my life."

"I'm not going to pay your scholarship bond back. You can pay back the money yourself, you fool."

I ignored my father's ranting. It was the first time I had defied my father. When, in 1962, I obtained a NSW Leaving Certificate and won a Teachers College scholarship, I applied for, and was offered a job in the Commonwealth Attorney General's Office. I applied for this job because I wanted to study law, but as a sixteen-year-old, I was too young to be admitted to law school at university. I intended to work for a year and then go to uni. My father bullied me into accepting the Teachers College scholarship to study economics at Sydney University. I loved and admired my father and wanted to be a lawyer like him.

"A cheap university education," he declared.

A week later I was at Batehaven on the New South Wales coast helping conduct a beach mission. Beach Mission was an organisation that operated in summer school holidays, on beaches near caravan parks, where forgiveness and everlasting life were offered to young children and teenagers. To parents, it offered the gift of free babysitting. One of the leaders of the beach mission team told me I should see if there was a job at Canberra Boys Grammar School.

I walked up the drive of the school in late January. I was awestruck by the winding drive, the tall trees, colonial buildings and extensive sporting fields; a far cry from the asphalt and ramshackle classrooms of Ashfield Boys High School.

I knocked unannounced on the door of Mr. Briggs, the deputy headmaster, a big man with very white hair, who appeared surprised to see me.

"I'm Russell Hodge. Jim Stephenson suggested I come and have a chat with you."

"Oh, Jim, how is he? Come on in." He smiled at me before retreating into his office.

"I am a teacher and I'm looking for a job. Is there a job that might come up?" I said.

"We only have one position to fill. We need a part-time economics, geography and divinity teacher. Other than that, we have no positions in the near future. What do you teach?"

"I'm a four-year trained high school economics and geography teacher. I have an economics degree from Sydney Uni and a Dip Ed. I'm also halfway through the SPTC course that will qualify me to be a Church of England minister."

The Lord moved in mysterious ways. I was hired on the spot. I immediately accepted enrolment in the ANU Law School and moved into Blaxland House in the grounds of the school as a boarding house master. I was responsible for twenty boys, so I was provided with food and shelter free of charge.

Boarding house masters were young; I was twenty-two years old. Ian Taylor was a boarding house master and about four years older than me. He was an Englishman and an experienced mountain climber. We developed a close friendship. Ian introduced me to rock climbing. We scaled the sheer cliffs of Mt. Piddington in the Blue Mountains. Ian climbed, anchored himself to the rock face. I climbed up to him, attached by a rope strapped to our waists. I was frightened but I absolutely trusted Ian to hold me if I slipped.

I taught part time and was enrolled in a full-time law course. I didn't teach divinity, but I gave sermons to the junior school on a fairly regular basis. The sermons were delivered in the school chapel. The chapel was a unique round, brick building built on sloping ground. The entrance to the chapel was where the ground was highest. As the ground fell away the brown brick chapel walls extended downwards in a circular manner to enclose the cavity created. This cavity, under the floor of the chapel, created a minister's retreat and storage area for religious paraphernalia.

When open, wide doors revealed pews stretching across the chapel facing the font at the other end. There were fewest pews at the entrance, and most pews in the middle, where the radius could be drawn. Opposite the entrance doors towards the far end of the chapel was a railing with a gap. This railing effectively separated the minister from the congregation. Just in front of the railing a metre from the walls of the chapel were two hidden staircases leading to the minister's retreat below.

I didn't like sermons. They reminded me of my mother's entreaties to wear shoes as I left home to walk to primary school. When I gave a sermon, I tried to do something different. On one occasion, I picked up a high stepladder from outside the chapel, and placed it in front of the rail. I delivered the sermon sitting on top of the ladder. The boys hung on to every word, wondering why I was on a ladder, and what would happen next.

Mr. Maffi was headmaster of the Junior School, which educated about one hundred and fifty boys. The chaplain was Guy Harrison. Guy was a very short man, thick set, upper class English and very proper. One day he approached me.

"Russell, in three weeks the Junior School is investing its prefects, and I would like you to give the sermon."

I didn't take it as a question so much as an order.

"One thing Russell—this is a very formal occasion, and all the prefects' parents will be there so your sermon must match the occasion."

"If it's so important, maybe you should get a minister, or even yourself to deliver the sermon."

Two elderly full-time, fully ordained Church of England ministers were part of the school staff.

"I want you to do it."

A week later Guy bailed me up again.

"Russell, remember that this sermon must reflect the occasion. I don't want any tricks."

"That's OK Guy, but if you want someone to stand up and pontificate to the boys to the point of stupefaction, the old fuddy duddies with white collars will do a better job than me."

"Remember what I said, no tricks."

I was very irritated when Guy bailed me up yet again to tell me what an important occasion it was. I again told him there were much more boring teachers than me qualified to give the sermon.

The day arrived. The boys filled the pews. The attendance was much greater than expected, and there was standing room only for parents around the walls of the chapel. Mr. Maffi sat on a chair against the wall to my left, and Guy on a chair against the wall to my right.

I stood in front of the railing facing the assembled

congregation. My sermon was on the god Baal and Elijah. The people of Israel turned to Baal, and Elijah returned from exile as prophet of the one true God. I explained this to the boys. Guy was very pleased. I saw him visibly relax as my monotone continued.

I raised my voice. "I, Elijah, challenge the gods of Baal."

From below the floor of the chapel came the words, "Who dares challenge the gods of Baal?"

Ian suddenly appeared from the gap where the stairs reached the chapel floor, and stood near me. He wore climbing boots, climbing trousers and jumper, ropes slung over his shoulder and TV rabbit ears on his head.

I said in a loud voice, "I challenge the gods of Baal."

By this time no boy was in his seat. They were all standing, their arms leaning on the pews in front.

"Who challenges the gods of Baal?" Ian yelled.

I motioned to the boys to join in.

"We challenge the gods of Baal," the boys and I shouted in unison.

Ian and I proceeded to conduct an extempore pantomime. The boys were standing and roaring. Ian challenged the boys. The boys and I yelled at Baal (Ian) to leave. After a few minutes we banished Baal, so he retreated down the stairs.

Mr. Maffi and Guy reacted differently. Guy was white while Mr. Maffi was bright red with rage.

I moved my arms in a downward fashion and the boys immediately sat down. I finished the sermon preaching the need to worship the one true God and not false idols. The boys sat in silence, transfixed by what I said, although it was pretty short. After the service ended Mr. Maffi and Guy stood at the door to say goodbye to the parents. I slunk past, but not before Mr. Maffi crooked his finger at me. I pretended not to notice.

I left the chapel and ran to the oval. The oval at the school was a large round playing field surrounded by mature English trees. There were tiers of grass retained by sandstone walls. I sat on a seat where Ian soon joined me.

"What was that about, you idiot?" I demanded.

"That was fun, wasn't it?" he replied.

"Yes, but you were supposed to come up, say one sentence and then disappear, not run a bloody pantomime. That's not what we agreed!"

"You started it," Ian said. "Anyway, what's the problem?"

"Guy told me the prefects were being invested, and I had to give a proper sermon with no tricks."

"You didn't tell me that."

"I know. I got carried away, but you weren't supposed to carry on."

We each, in our own space, contemplated the situation.

"You know Mr. Maffi is probably heading for Mr. McKeown's office right now, and we are going to be out of a job," Ian remarked. Paul McKeown was the headmaster of Canberra Grammar School, our employer.

"I know."

We sat in silence. Suddenly Ian was his old cheerful self.

"It's not all bad. You will lose your job but I won't lose mine. I didn't make any promises to Guy."

I sat in silence.

He added, "What will you do for a job? Your father will give you money, won't he?"

"I am sure he will, if I can get pigs to fly."

I sat and contemplated my future. I could always work in a bar. Life normally took care of itself. I was in God's hands.

I sat with Ian. The soft Canberra winter sun fell on my face. The air was still. I felt a bond with my friend, a bond created by shared experiences, shared danger, and a reliance on each other.

I was calm, relaxed and at peace with the world.

The dreaded axe failed to materialise. Over the next few days I saw Guy in the distance and managed to avoid him. When I did bump into him, I understood why I still had a job. The parents were the first to leave the chapel after my sermon and it took a long time for them to depart. Virtually every parent congratulated Mr. Maffi and Guy on the service, and raved about how entertaining my sermon was. It was a win-win. The boys were entertained, the parents loved it, Mr. Maffi and Guy bathed in my reflected glory, and I never delivered another sermon at Canberra Boys Grammar School.

In some ways I felt sad sitting in Mme Renault's class. I disliked the disrespect she was shown by the students. I understood why they were restless and inattentive but students never seem to comprehend how their behaviour could impact on a teacher. In my first year at Sydney Uni, we had a young inexperienced lecturer. He was hopeless. We students called out in class, interrupted him, ridiculed him—made it impossible for him to teach. He hung himself in the university toilets mid-way through the semester. I felt guilty that we might have killed him. Mme Renault was far more competent than the Sydney Uni lecturer, however I was acutely aware of how she might be feeling, and I didn't like it.

Twelve

As the university semester marched on, my studying hours increased. I started earlier and worked longer. I now frequented the restaurant and bar on the corner, less than fifty metres from where I lived. It's not that I particularly liked it, but it opened early and I could grab a cup of coffee before studying or heading off to uni.

A barmaid, Danielle, a university graduate served me. She decreed that she was my unofficial French teacher. I was struggling with my studies and desperately wanted to pass. Paradoxically, I had no difficulty pursuing other activities outside of uni study even though I was worried that I'd fail.

I talked to Danielle about the homeless. She gave me an article from *Le Parisien*. The article described the life of a young mother with two young children. She was destitute and living in Paris, each night moving to a different shelter. Some nights she slept with her children in the corridors of apartments. Hers was not an isolated case as homelessness in Paris was endemic. Part of the problem arose from the expansion of the European Economic Community. Countries such as Romania, Poland and Bulgaria became member nations and these countries had significant poverty. Freedom of movement within the EEC allowed people with no future and no hope to move to France. These people were not entitled to welfare payments from the French government. The result was that thousands of people simply changed their place of poverty. Even worse, they abandoned family and social networks that provided a sense of community and emotional support. Their only means of support was the kindness of strangers giving them money.

I was very moved by the article and asked Danielle if there was a way I could be involved in helping the destitute. She suggested I contact Emmaus, a long-established charity that aided the disadvantaged. She said that they were always looking for volunteers so I went to the nearest Emmaus store to join the charity. I was directed to an office in the city. I reached the main office and lined up to fill in the form to be a volunteer. An older man looked at my answers, asked me some questions, and said I was not a suitable candidate. I was not in Paris long enough to go through the assessment and training program, and my French wasn't good enough.

I wasted half a day trying to volunteer for the charity. The doors of opportunity kept closing. This spur-of-the-moment, bizarre idea didn't reach fruition.

I told Damien about it over dinner that night. In English as usual, Damien said he had a friend who did volunteer work in hospitals, and he would arrange for me to meet her.

"When are you going to ask her?" I asked.

"In the next couple of days."

"What about ringing her now?"

"Life doesn't revolve around you, you know."

"I'm well aware of that, but you'll get busy and forget about it."

Damien sighed in exasperation. He rang his friend, and arranged for us to have dinner the next Saturday night.

That weekend, I followed Damien to Gare de L'Est and I knew that we were going to the fourth arrondissement. I walked with Damien who nattered away in English, oblivious to my surroundings. The only thing I remembered was a shop we passed set back from the road. A girl, probably a teenager, was staggering outside the shop probably drunk or high. I looked at her and momentarily slowed down. Damien looked at her and continued without the slightest change of pace. He was a man on a mission.

We eventually came to a typical Parisian street. There were rows of apartments four storeys high that stretched from one block to the next. There were no gardens in front of the apartments—they all abutted the footpath. Even though there were rows of identical buildings the streetscape was very attractive. The Parisian landscape of wide streets and rows of trees changed what would otherwise be boring sameness into attractive ambience. We walked past door after door—the only differences being the colours of the doors and the numbers above.

Damien suddenly veered to the left and moved towards a door. He rang the bell. The door opened and we walked into a small foyer with a narrow set of stairs. There was no lift in the building so we wound our way up to the fourth floor where Maraise lived.

It was a loft. Maraise was a big well-dressed woman probably in her late fifties. She had a hunched back, bad knees and had lived alone in the apartment for fifteen years. I couldn't imagine how she managed the stairs each day. Damien was breathing heavily when we reached the top of the stairs and had to catch his breath before he entered the apartment.

The apartment was tiny. It was right at the top of the building, and was wedged under a sloping roof with a huge beam across the ceiling. I moved straight into the tiny kitchen with adjacent eating space. Maraise suggested I sit in the lounge room, a space with room for only three chairs. I moved to the lounge room and hit my head on the timber beam. I didn't visit the bedroom or bathroom but they must have been equally tiny.

Damien and Maraise started to chat in French. Damien had already warned me that Maraise didn't speak English so I wouldn't get much out of the visit.

I sat in the lounge room absorbing the surroundings and listening, without much understanding of the conversation between Damien and Maraise. Their conversation seemed to be gossip relating to mutual acquaintances.

After a while Damien announced, "Dinner is served."

These were the last English words spoken until after we left the apartment.

Damien opened a bottle of red wine and Maraise served coq au vin with a side dish of mushrooms, beans and tomatoes.

Maraise's mouth was in perpetual motion. Its motion was very fast. Although she made no attempt to ensure I understood her, I was able to catch the gist of what she was saying. Maraise didn't use ten words if the same idea or subject could be expressed in a hundred words. I asked her questions and she answered the question in one way and then repeated the answer with different words.

Maraise worked for a charity in a hospital. Unlike Australia, hospitals in Paris provided food and shelter for the destitute and needy, but the hospital at St. Denis had had to close its doors to the destitute as it ran out of resources. Marais worked as a volunteer in the hospital on a casual basis. Her work involved talking to people in desperate need. She provided advice and moral support.

I thought I could do this and Maraise said she would arrange for me to come to the hospital to help. I was very happy. Maraise talked and talked and over a number of hours I learnt much about the difficulties of housing immigrants. She talked about how they were given hotel rooms which were then trashed. She was sympathetic but very critical of some of the behaviours she experienced.

Over the next three weeks I pressed Damien as to when Maraise would take me to the hospital so I could help. Damien told me that Maraise was sick and had gone to the country, and she had to ask her boss. The excuses rolled out time after time. I eventually gave up asking.

Thirteen

Despite my academic difficulties I still went to the gym near St. Michelle. I was walking down Rue St. Michelle after a gym session, just after I had met Maraise, when a young woman approached me asking for money for her baby.

I brusquely rebutted her request. I walked two steps and stopped. I looked at her. Although she was better dressed than other street beggars, she still looked quite nondescript. She didn't appear to have the physical and mental disabilities that were apparent in other persons demanding money on the rues of Paris.

"What do you want?" I asked.
"I want money for food for my baby."
"Where's your baby?"
"She's being looked after by my mother."
"Do you speak English?"
"Non."

On an impulse I said I would pay her ten euros if she would have a cup of coffee with me. I rationalised this rash offer as an opportunity to improve my French.

Life was pretty desperate when I had to pay someone to talk to me! C'est la vie. I had considered this before. I thought I could put a notice on the student noticeboard. "Friend wanted, little old man, very sociable, can't speak French." I wasn't sure that it would have much appeal to students at the Sorbonne.

The woman led me to an outside table at a nearby bar restaurant. We sat down. The first thing I noticed was her purple boots. She sat more or less sideways in the chair, and her feet protruded from under the edge of the table. The bright purple boots covered her ankles but I could still see the holes in the soles of the boots. She appeared to be mid-twenties and wore a pale blue, long dress. Over her blouse she wore a dark blue jumper. She was solidly built, had long black hair, olive skin and a prominent nose. The jumper she was wearing clung, and gave definition, to her large upper arms. It flapped loosely at her wrist as she pulled out a cigarette and started to smoke.

I gave her ten euros and told her she could leave whenever she wanted. We started to communicate. The most common words spoken in the next half hour were "Vous comprenez?"

Her name was Brenda. From her clear and slowly spoken French I learnt she had two children, one six months old and the other two years, was divorced, and lived in a truck with her mother. She answered my questions without emotion, but I suspected the apparent hesitation in her speech was to make sure I understood what she was saying. I doubted the truth of her discourse, perhaps arising from cynicism that formed part of my lawyer's armoury, or perhaps I was prejudiced due to her economic circumstance.

It was an excellent introduction to my studies. Descartes postulated that knowledge was only those things that were beyond doubt; if Descartes were present he would say whatever I was acquiring wasn't knowledge. She had no job, no means of support, and came from Romania, the latter the only 'fact' that constituted knowledge.

When I asked her how she survived, she said that she ate by extracting food from garbage bins. This intrigued me. In my last semester at Sydney Uni, I studied gaspillage. The study was in the context of feeding the poor and homeless from waste thrown out by supermarkets. She asked me if I had eaten food from a garbage bin. I said I hadn't but if she did, I would do the same.

The conversation was slow and repetitious as I wanted to understand everything she said. I asked if I could be with her when she hunted for food out of garbage bins. She said she would show me but she wanted money, seven hundred euros to buy a caravan. I offered her half the cost of a tennis lesson, twenty euros, which after much hesitation she accepted. We agreed to meet at Gare de Pierrefitte - Stains at three o'clock the next Sunday afternoon.

That night I recounted my meeting with Brenda to Damien. He looked at me. I couldn't understand his demeanour; I was not used to seeing his frown deepen and his face became red so quickly.

"Don't be a fool." He raised his voice. "She will meet you at the station. She will not be alone, she will have another woman with her. They will take you to a place where there are deserted and derelict buildings. You will go to her truck and you will be bashed and robbed."

"Okay, okay! I can hear you."

"Don't you know only yesterday a woman was pushed under a train? The area is very violent. There are huge numbers of unemployed young thugs. Promise me you won't go. Promise me!" Damien's voice was one level below shouting.

"Of course, I won't go," I said. "I would be stupid if I went."

"If you must deal with homeless or beggars at least stay in Paris. Don't go outside Paris."

I don't like being shouted at—I get stressed. When I am shouted at, I don't comprehend what is being said, I emotionally defend myself by pushing very hard against what is being said. If Damien had expressed his views calmly and logically, I would have taken a great deal of notice of what he said. As it was, I dismissed what he said as irrational ranting. More's the pity as he was uncannily prescient.

Fourteen

Madame Blanc-Benon was my art teacher. Her lectures lasted one and a half hours once a week. The art class by Sorbonne standards was relatively small with about twenty students. The students were overwhelmingly female.

Every lecture I occupied the same space, halfway down the class near the window. Three young women sat in the front row. There were no other students between us. Six weeks of lectures passed and my understanding of the lectures was very limited.

I had a general policy of asking questions in class. I knew that some students would hold me in silent contempt because of my ignorance. When I first started the course, I asked students if they spoke English and the invariable answer was "No." Gradually the ability of French students to speak English improved. Now when I asked students if they spoke English most said "Yes," and those not confident in English referred me to a student who did.

When I asked questions in the art class, Mme Blanc-Benon answered patiently. She was probably mid-thirties, dressed in a conservative middle-class manner. She was ordinary in a really nice way. I felt comfortable in her class as she had an appearance of caring for students. On occasions at the start of the break in class she answered my questions in English.

I was fortunate that other students had the same attitude. Often, after I asked a question and looked blankly at Mme Blanc-Benon, a student behind me explained in English. After one class I was walking down the stairs on my way home. A young woman walked beside me. I recognised her from my class but I had never spoken to her before.

We had a conversation in French.

"How are you coping with the French language?" she asked.

"I find it very difficult."

"Your French is very poor. Did you pass a government exam to qualify for the Sorbonne?"

The words were frank and harsh but the manner in which they were spoken was kind and sympathetic.

"No, I didn't do an exam. I am a Sydney University exchange student."

She asked me why I was at the Sorbonne studying philosophy. This was a common question I was asked by French students. Almost every student that spoke to me wanted to know why I was at the Sorbonne.

I always said, "I really like philosophy. The Sorbonne is the best university in the world to study philosophy." It was a short explanation that didn't require further questions. French students loved to be told their university was the best in the world. Of course, the eighteenth-century philosopher Emmanuel Kant would not have been pleased. Kant believed the supreme law of morality is based on the categorical imperative. This meant you can "act only on that maxim through which you can at the same time will that it should become a universal law."

You cannot tell a lie. If a murderer with a gun came to your house and said, "Is your mother inside? I want to kill her," Kant stated you could not say "no" if you knew she was inside the house.

Ironically, and paradoxically perhaps, I believed the Sorbonne was the best university in the world to study philosophy. Kant's displeasure would have arisen from my motivation to keep myself and other students happy. Kant required me to answer the question solely and only from the perspective of truth. I was both telling the truth, and intentionally giving French students pride in their university. The motivation to give the students a sense of pride means my answer didn't meet the categorical imperative. It was therefore not a moral act.

Another view was that of a consequentialist position. This was normative ethical theory. It stated that the consequences of what we did were the ultimate basis for any judgement of what was right or wrong. Some called it an ends-justify-the-means philosophy. If I lied to the murderer, he went away and my mother was saved; telling the lie was an ethical, or moral, act. My answer to the students was normative consequentialism.

We all lived our lives either consciously or subconsciously according to a moral code. Mine was clear. I lived by the code that suited my purpose at the time. In answering students' questions, I was a consequentialist. When I asked my children, "Who crashed my car?" I was a Kant devotee; truth was king.

To enter the Sorbonne to study philosophy, students must pass the baccalaureate at the end of high school. Philosophy was a compulsory subject. All students studying philosophy at the Sorbonne started the semester with a background in this discipline. This was not the case at Sydney University. I had studied Ethics, Art and Reality. This was a very popular first-year course. Over a thousand students studied it. It was sheer entertainment and lecturers received a standing ovation at the end of the course.

My art tutor then was Laura. It was her first year as a tutor. She was very like my daughter Vanessa. She had the same petite build, the same mousy coloured hair and was of a similar height. Like Ness, she was very clever. The tutorials were small and entertaining.

Laura projected an image on a screen.

She said to me, "Is this a work of art?"

"Where is it?"

"Why is that relevant?" she asked.

"Because 'My Bed' by Tracy Emin is only art because it is in a gallery," I retorted. This piece of 'art' was displayed in the Tate Gallery. It was an actual unmade bed surrounded by detritus.

"Andy Warhol's Brillo boxes are art, no matter where they are," she replied.

My old age brought cynicism and I suspected a trap. Her expression mirrored expressions I had seen on Ness's face. I knew obstinacy when I saw it.

"So, is it art?"

"You give me your definition of art and I will tell you whether it is art or not."

"No, you provide me with your definition of art, and then tell me whether or not, in accordance with your definition, it is art."

She was like my daughter; she was not going away.

"It is art," I reluctantly said, knowing it was a trap.

She turned to other students. It was very exciting sitting in a classroom with about a dozen really clever young minds. The students' enthusiasm, the depth of discussion, and differing opinions made time pass very quickly. The consensus was that the image shown was art. Laura then disclosed that the image was taken from a part of the exterior of the Mitchell Library. It was not art.

Laura's tutorials lasted for an hour. They were supposed to finish at one p.m., lunchtime but her tutorials always extended into the lunch hour. Tutorials at the Sorbonne were never extended. Except to a limited extent there was never any discussion, or real interaction between teacher and student.

A month after lectures started Romain telephoned me. He said he had some friends working in a contemporary art gallery and would I like to see it? I accepted his invitation.

We caught the train and arrived at the gallery. I didn't notice the name of it. There was an open area with a glass roof adjacent to the gallery. Romain was a very handsome young man and I assumed women found him attractive. We approached the open area and three young women walked quickly towards us. Seeing the young women greeting Romain was like watching bees plucking pollen from an open flower. I stood beside him like a dead stalk. He introduced me to his friends and we entered the gallery.

There were no paintings. The exhibition consisted of mainly metal sculptures and a light show. The objects were displayed randomly throughout the gallery, their interest heightened by the use of lights and contrast.

I learnt without knowing I learnt. I understood without knowing I understood.

Mme Banc-Benon taught the philosophy of art, the foundation of art being Plato's mimesis. This basis was modified or disputed by Aristotle and Hegel. I was unaware that subconsciously attitudes and information were being inculcated within me. Similarly, Laura's tutorials had heightened my awareness, and made me think of art.

Before I went to the Sorbonne I didn't frequent art galleries. I couldn't remember when I last walked inside a gallery. I wasn't interested in paintings or art. I walked into the gallery with Romain and I looked at the pieces. I considered what they represented. I didn't see the pieces of metal as mere objects. Something within me evoked emotions as I analysed the shapes, the forms, the texture.

I was not conscious of the process whereby I appreciated art, but there was a process. I looked at a work of art and asked myself what it was about, or what it represented. Next I asked myself how I felt. It was like sitting on a psychiatrist's couch. In this way art became deeply personal. I found abstract art more difficult to interpret. The shaped metal objects Romain showed me didn't have context, however they did have texture, form and interest. As I looked at these metal pieces I brought them within myself. Sharp-edged objects made me feel threatened and nervous, with rounded objects I was calm. My appreciation of the works was extremely rudimentary; however I did think about my inner feelings, and why I felt like I did. Feeling threatened represented my struggle against the weight of my own expectations to do well. Calmness was being with Romain and his friends, away from the real world.

Fifteen

Some of my best opportunities to speak French were right under my nose. Danielle had taken an interest in my education and introduced me to two middle-aged women who regularly patronised the bar. They talked to me about their life, particularly their financial problems. People struggled wherever they were.

One of the more enjoyable learning experiences from Danielle came after an outing with Romain. Romain had popped in to visit his father, and asked me if I would like to go with him to the football. I responded positively, and his father invited himself along. France was playing Japan in soccer. I soon realised we weren't going to see football, we were going to watch the soccer.

I dutifully followed Damien as we walked to Gare du Nord and then caught RER D to Gare du Stadt de France. The Stadt de France was a long walk from the station but walking and chatting swallowed time and distance. Damien was amiably nattering in English in my ear. Time was passing slowly. I switched off and enjoyed the streetscape. We passed office buildings. I enjoyed the wide tree-lined streets and high-rise office towers with unique architectural differences. Different shapes, colours, unusual alignment, open spaces, reed swamps, gardens and an unusual sports area made the walk interesting and pleasant.

After eventually reaching the huge stadium we walked all the way around to the other side of it. Romain was in a crowded bar and eatery with a group of his friends. He had the tickets to the game, and we walked up the stairs into the stadium. He was an impecunious young man so we watched the game from the upper reaches at the back of the stadium.

I sat away from Romain, in the middle of his friends. They sat beside, behind and in front of me.

The young man beside me asked in English, "Do you want to speak English or French?"

"Francais s'il vous plait."

I soon learnt the language of football. Romain's friends told me words for offside, free kick, goal, throw-in and penalty. The game was fantastic, but little did I know I was to witness a national catastrophe. Japan beat France 1–0.

I bought *Le Parisien* the next day as I always did. Huge banner headlines reported the defeat. Acres of newsprint detailed the failings of the French team.

I sauntered into the corner restaurant the next day, ordered my coffee as usual and said to Danielle, "The football result last night was very interesting."

"It was terrible!" she said. "The French team were hopeless."

"No, they weren't! They were good."

"How would you know?" She was showing anger.

"I was there, I saw the game." I was oblivious to her body language and tone of her voice. I continued, "The French team was brilliant. They played well above their ability, they were just beaten by a better team and more talented players."

She looked at me with absolute contempt. I didn't understand the diatribe that followed but I knew it ended with a description of the quality of Australian soccer with her thumbs jabbing toward the ground.

Of course, some of my most enjoyable sporting experiences were due to who I was with and the circumstances as much as the game itself. I enjoyed the soccer game with Romain, but the best part was being surrounded by his friends and the way they interacted with me. A minor game can be just as enjoyable as a major event.

Robert, general manager of a large corporation, and I liked to watch the St. George rugby league team. We sat on the grass at Kogarah oval. It was 1980. Robert was dapperly dressed in a crisply ironed striped shirt, beige sports trousers and a half-length trench coat, which he laid on the grass so we could sit on it. About ten minutes before the start of the game against Manly, I spotted a familiar face ten metres away.

"Hey Ratso," I yelled out.

Ratso turned in my direction, squinted, smiled and raised his arm in recognition as he walked towards me.

"Do you know him?" Robert asked incredulously. "He's not a friend of yours, is he?"

'He' was a man my age, wearing old trousers, a football jumper that had seen better day, and streamers hanging from his shoulders. He was medium height and build, with a mop of uncombed black hair—washed maybe three weeks ago—casually swept across his forehead. An old bag and a money pouch were slung around his waist. I was relieved that at least he had put in his false teeth—sometimes he didn't bother.

"How's the milk run going Ratso?"

"Pretty good—you and Craig only lost half me business."

"Very funny. How come you're selling streamers?"

"Me and Sue make them during the week, get in here for nothin, bludge free hotdogs and watch the footy. I'd better get goin, save me a spot will ya."

"How could you have lost half his business?" asked Robert. Before I could answer Robert continued. "Is he a milkman? Who is Craig? Did you drink all his milk?" Too many questions and too little time, but Robert insisted I answer.

I wasn't in my law practice very long when my secretary told me that a Mrs. Ratcliffe wanted to see me without an appointment. I was very busy as I was in the middle of doing my nails.

I hadn't seen Sue Ratcliffe for over five years. We both went to the fellowship at St. Paul's, Oatley and Sue was Ratso's girlfriend. I loved Sue, not in a romantic way, but for the person she was. She was always friendly, bubbly, great company and a joy to be around. Ian 'Ratso' Ratcliffe and myself regularly played touch football in Oatley Park.

Sue was very distressed. They had bought a milk run and Ian was standing between the trailer and the back of the car when a car rammed into the trailer from behind seriously injuring him. Sue wanted to know what she needed to do legally.

I asked her what was happening to the milk run while Ian was injured.

"Craig's doing it."

I knew Craig from fellowship days.

After Sue left, I gave Craig a ring and asked how he was managing being a milkman. He said it was tough because he had a full-time job and I asked him if I could help.

After that, I got up at three o'clock in the morning three days a week and drove the Porsche to Villawood with my work clothes packed. I picked up Ratso's milk truck and drove to the dairy where I loaded the truck with crates of milk.

"I'll make this as simple as possible. You're a solicitor, so you're not going to collect money," Craig said as he started my milk run training.

The run was in a relatively flat area with row upon row of fibro houses. Villawood was a working-class suburb. Not everyone wanted milk. I drove down the street, stopped and looked at the empty bottles on or near a fence. I simply picked up an empty bottle and replaced it with a full bottle of milk. Sometimes there was a note when someone wanted extra or less. At the end of the run I took the trailer back to the depot and unloaded the crates. Like all milkmen I did a lot of running.

I went back to my parent's place where I had a shower and changed, then either went to the office or straight to court. I became fit very quickly, and really enjoyed the work. After four months, Ian completely recovered and took back the run.

About ten minutes after the game started, Robert spotted Ratso and moved over to make room for him on his coat. Ratso sat down.

"You were lucky you only lost half your business," Robert remarked. I knew I was among friends, who were quite happy to have a joke at my expense.

The game became of little consequence as Robert, Ratso and I enjoyed each other's company. Robert and Ratso lived on different ends of the socio-economic spectrum. Their education, wealth and family situations (Robert was a bachelor) were foreign to each other. We had a common interest in St. George rugby league team. I was the link that provided the environment for animated exchanges, mostly at my expense. The game was a cracker—St. George won, and we parted company with big smiles on our faces.

My regular visits to the corner restaurant bar and my banter with Danielle continued until mid-November. Barmaids, like the homeless, are itinerant. One day she was there, next day she was gone. I doubt that Danielle understood she was an important part of my life, not that she had any reason to know this, nor did she have any responsibility to me. I wasn't her child but I still missed her.

Sixteen

The badminton sessions lasted two hours and were always physically demanding. For the next six weeks I practised with Jacques who was my standard and actually asked me to play with him. The class was very competitive. I was ranked seventeenth out of thirty-six. Sabine was ranked fifth and the number one woman. The sessions were structured; there was the warm up, skills training—which I didn't always enjoy—and free playing.

In the third week Le Prof asked me to participate in a demonstration. He positioned me on one side of the net and positioned two of the better players on the other side of the net. He then proceeded to give me instructions. I didn't understand a word he was saying but the session was going nicely. The good players were hitting the *ballon* to me and I was consistently returning it back over the net. Suddenly for no apparent reason Le Prof started yelling at me.

"TROP COURT RUSSELL, TROP COURT RUSSELL, TROP COURT RUSSELL!"

I knew this was "too short Russell". Yelling at me was disrespectful. I thought it was unfair, I already knew I was very short. I was upset that he was making a public point of me being vertically challenged. He was yelling other words I didn't understand—he repeated them three times. Jacques motioned for me to leave the court. When I moved from the court the yelling stopped. He then called for Sabine to take my place and I watched her play. How was I supposed to know he wanted me to hit the *ballon* to the back of the court! *C'est ridiculous*!!!

Le Prof ruled with a rod of iron without fear or favour. On one occasion, he explained how to play a particular stroke and how tactically it could be used. I presumed that was what he was saying, he was moving about the court playing an imaginary shot while speaking, what to me, was gibberish. All the students were standing in a group watching the professor when a young woman left the group and headed for the door of the gym. As the woman neared the door, Le Prof stopped, turned and looked towards her. The gymnasium was totally silent except for the soft steps of the departing woman. He loudly called out to her.

"Where do you think you're going?" I presume this is what he said from the student's reply.

"To the bathroom, Sir."

"No, you're not. Come back here."

Thirty-five students and Le Prof watched in total silence as she sheepishly walked back to the group, where for the next five minutes she uncomfortably hopped from one leg to the other. When Le Prof finished his demonstration, the bathroom was declared open. There was no gender inequality at the Sorbonne.

I enjoyed playing with Jacques. I was improving my listening and speaking skills without realising it. I travelled on the Metro with Jacques after each session. Jacques lived in the suburbs with his parents and it was his second year at university. He asked me about Australia and how I was coping with the course. He was not in any of my classes. It was my first personal contact of any depth with a student at the Sorbonne. I found the language issues associated with playing badminton far more challenging than any other area. When instructions were given in French I had to understand and react. To do otherwise caused issues. Passive listening or social chatting in French was much easier.

What I had also learnt was that the so-called 'soft option' of badminton had the same level of integrity as every other course at the Sorbonne. Nothing was easy. Nobody cut me any slack; I was just another student. As it should have been.

I really enjoyed the badminton sessions yet the environment in which I was playing was totally foreign. I was not used to the authoritarianism or discipline. I played competitive sport most of my life—baseball, cricket, tennis, rugby—but never under conditions like those imposed by Le Prof, with perhaps one exception, albeit to a lesser extent.

In my early thirties, I was sitting at my desk in my legal practice when I received a call from my friend John. I spent four years at university with John doing an economics degree and teachers college diploma.

"Hi Russ. I'm captain of St. Paul's Kogarah Methodist cricket team," John said. "We're short of players, and I was wondering if you'd like to play?"

"What grade are you playing?" I said.

"C."

"So you want me to play C grade in a churches' comp?" I sniffed.

"We don't have a D grade."

He then went on to explain the strict dress rules. I must wear cricket whites or creams and white boots or sandshoes.

The following Saturday I arrived late at the game. I parked my Porsche and noticed play had already started. Our opponents were fielding, we were batting. I recognised the umpire. John spotted me.

"You will need to change into your cricket gear."

"I am in my cricket gear."

I was wearing blue shorts, a crumpled T-shirt and old blue gym shoes. John looked at me and shrugged his shoulders. I had a very busy legal practice and after John's phone call I did not consider what to wear. When I went to get dressed to go to the game I realised I didn't have any cricket clothes. I didn't have a choice as to what I was to wear.

It was soon my turn to bat and I started to walk onto the field. The umpire called out "Stop." Then, "Captain, I want to speak to you." The umpire was a man in his seventies. He wore an immaculate white umpire's coat, black trousers, black shoes and carried the usual paraphernalia associated with umpiring a cricket game. His distinguishing feature was his limp. The team called him "Hoppy" behind his back.

John walked out to meet the umpire. John was a big man—not only was his build imposing but he had a certain presence and air of authority. He wore a cream flannel shirt, regulation trousers, stained at the groin where he rubbed the ball to keep it shiny and, of course, proper lace-up cricket boots.

I stood nearby and listened to their conversation. Hoppy told John that I wasn't correctly attired and that he wouldn't let me bat.

"That's a great shame, ump. His father abused him as a kid. I met him at Kings Cross. He lives on the street. He has no money, no clothes. St. Vincent de Paul gave him his shoes and shorts. He is a terrible cricketer, but as Christians we thought we should ask him to play with us. I can understand it is more important to Jesus that he wears the right clothes than receive our compassion. After all, rules are rules," John said.

I strongly resented John saying I was a terrible cricketer. I noticed he smirked when he said it. Hoppy of course relented.

I walked to the crease and took guard. In church cricket there was only one umpire, who stood at the bowler's end of the wicket. I looked down the wicket at Hoppy and saw him look at me quizzically. I continued to bat for about ten minutes and from time to time, when I was not batting, I stood beside Hoppy at the bowler's end. I avoided speaking to him.

Our perceptions always exist in context. We can know someone really well in a business or sporting environment but when we see that person in a different context we don't recognise him. It is about being present and aware. I often walked along Berrara Beach, thoughts rolling around in my head, totally unaware of the wind, waves or features on the beach. I lived life in my head not here on earth. If we were truly present and aware, the context in which we saw and met people wouldn't matter. We would recognise them irrespective of the circumstances.

I stood beside Hoppy and we looked at each other. I smiled and I saw the dawn of recognition cross his face.

"You're not homeless," he cried. "You're my solicitor."

With that he rapidly limped his way to the boundary to accost John.

"He is not homeless—he's my solicitor," he shouted.

"In that case if he hasn't sent you a bill I suggest you be nice to him—you know what solicitors are like," John replied.

Hoppy calmed down and returned to his umpire's post. Over the next twenty minutes we chatted amicably about the upcoming sale of his house and purchase of an apartment.

On a couple of occasions he adjudged me to be not out, when I was clearly out.

Three weeks before the game I had met Frank (Hoppy) and his wife in my office. We spent forty-five minutes discussing in detail the sale of his house, and his purchase of another property. It was not a casual conversation. Of course, I gave Frank a big discount on his legal fees.

Frank and Le Prof had much in common. They were both authoritarian and sticklers for the rules. At the Sorbonne I learnt to do as I was told, obey the rules and follow the process, as there was no alternative. There was no John to change the rules.

Seventeen

"Where are you going?"

Damien had never asked me before. It was the Sunday afternoon that I had arranged to meet Brenda. I had been studying all day. I didn't have a bag, the only things I carried were fifty euros and my Navigo pass for identification.

"Just for a walk," I said. "I need a rest."

I walked out the door thinking that if I wanted a mother I wouldn't be in Paris.

Like a teenage boy intent on deceiving his parents, I was well prepared. I had to walk to Gare du Nord and find RER D to travel to Pierrefitte - Stains. I hoped the Navigo card took me to the suburbs of Paris.

The Navigo card worked. I arrived at Pierrefitte - Stains station about five minutes late. There was only one exit and I walked towards it. Unlike the Paris Metro I had to tap my Navigo card on the machine to exit the station. I walked through the gates and immediately saw a paved area, a narrow rue and a small attractive garden. Its dominant features were large trees, shrubs and pretty flowers scattered in beds throughout the garden. The trees and shrubs camouflaged the large blocks of flats peeping between the branches of the trees. To my right was a pharmacy and supermarket.

I was looking forward to the adventure. Brenda was going to show me how to scavenge for food. I wouldn't be listening to a lecture on gaspillage at Sydney University, I would be living the lecture.

Brenda, holding the hand of a very young child, approached and I walked to meet her. She was wearing the same clothes as when we met. I particularly noticed the purple boots and dark blue jumper. She was not wearing a coat and seemed cold. Oddly she had someone with her.

"Bonjour," I said.

"Bonjour. This is my sister."

She gestured towards the young woman beside her. She was much younger than Brenda, thinner and had blonde hair. She was also better dressed. I particularly noticed her bright coloured clothes. Her dress and youth gave an air of optimism that was not apparent in Brenda. Brenda looked towards the toddler.

"This is my daughter," she said.

"Where's your baby?"

"She's being looked after by a friend."

It was pleasant but not friendly. I was not introduced to her sister or daughter by name, only by relationship. We approached a waiting bus. I told Brenda I would pay for her and her sister and asked how much it was.

Brenda jumped up the stairs of the side door halfway down the bus. "We don't pay, we're gypsies!"

I sat on one side of the bus and the two gypsies sat adjacent to me on the other side of the bus. We travelled in silence through the suburbs of Paris for about twenty minutes.

Finally Brenda stood up. Nothing was said and I followed her and her sister down the steps of the bus onto the footpath.

Brenda strode ahead. I noticed that we were in what I thought was a place. It was a large square where various roads met, typical of Paris, even in the suburbs.

Brenda's sister told me the name of the place but it didn't register, other than it was a town square. I immediately forgot the name.

We crossed the square and Brenda led us down a narrow street, barely visible from the other side of the square. We continued down the lane, turned into another lane then another lane. On either side of the lane were multi-storey derelict buildings, ostensibly uninhabited. They were daubed with graffiti, windows were broken, rooves were damaged, exterior paint was peeling or non-existent. The buildings were surrounded by broken bitumen or concrete strewn with papers, leaves and garbage. I had a slight sense of unease as we meandered through a wasteland of hopelessness and poverty. The most remarkable aspect was there was no one else in sight. We walked for twenty minutes and didn't see a single person.

As we were walking Brenda carried her daughter. Brenda held her away from her. When her child said something in Romanian Brenda brought her close to her face and the little girl kissed her mother. They were playing a game. The game was repeated again and again.

"What is your daughter saying?" I asked.

"Encore!"

I saw Brenda differently. I saw a young mother who loved her daughter, with her child responding to the love and affection. This love between mother and daughter transcended poverty, race and way of life.

The game eventually ended. "You look cold," I said. "Where's your coat?"

"I don't have one."

"Can I carry your daughter?" I asked in my best French.

Brenda passed her daughter to me and I held her in my arms as we walked through the wasteland of derelict buildings. I no longer noticed my surroundings, I felt calm as Brenda's daughter put her arms around my neck with her body nestled across my chest.

It wasn't long before I got tired. I realised how strong Brenda was, as I found the toddler quite heavy. Fortunately, perhaps sensing my fatigue, the toddler wanted to be with her mother. With some relief, I passed her back to Brenda. My French was limited so our conversation was rudimentary. I learnt her sister was eighteen years old and lived with her boyfriend.

After what seemed quite a long walk we approached an open area. It appeared to be a bitumen cul-de-sac. I had no idea where I was. As we approached I noticed there were puddles in the road from the recent heavy rain. Brenda nonchalantly strolled past three women washing clothes in the puddles. There were half a dozen caravans scattered randomly throughout the open area. They were close to each other but sufficiently far apart to give the caravan occupants a modicum of privacy. I was momentarily distracted. The appearance of caravans in the middle of suburbia was totally unexpected. It was strange, but I sensed the roar of the ocean and the smell of salt sea air even though I was very much inland. In a perverse sort of way, the caravans reminded me of Berrara Beach.

I was ten years old when my parents first took me to Berrara, an isolated hamlet on the New South Wales South Coast. My father and his friends were the advance party. They took the twelve-by-twelve-foot tents for their families, together with chairs, tables, eating and cooking utensils. In between drinking copious amounts of alcohol, they erected the tents. A few days later my father and mother and six children drove to Berrara, cramped inside our old Holden; five kids in the back, two adults and a child in the front and no seatbelts.

Berrara was a three-hour drive from Sydney. The last six and a half miles were on a winding bush dirt road. Magnificent gum trees hugged the edge of the road that gave way to a flood plain decorated with Christmas Bells and various multi-coloured wildflowers. When flood or bushfire hit Berrara, it was totally isolated.

Berrara Road ended at the camping ground on the headland owned by the Kirpsons. It was bounded on the western side by Berrara Creek and on the eastern side by the Pacific Ocean. To the south across the creek was Berrara Beach. It was idyllic. I played with the Baines and Whittaker kids, and we roamed the park playing hide and seek, chasings, and of course swimming and playing in the creek every day.

The living conditions were primitive. There was no water, no sewerage and no electricity. The amenities amounted to a shed containing a pit toilet. It was my job to fetch the water. I carried empty kerosene tins to the underground tank. On the top of the tank was a pipe with a hole in the top and a handle. I put water in the hole in the pipe and pumped until water spouted from the end of the pipe. I then filled the kerosene tin and carried it full of water two hundred yards to our tent. The water was used for washing up and for Mum to have a shower. Light at night consisted of two hurricane lamps. We ate and went to bed early. If I wanted to read, the light was impossibly dull.

After a few years, my father built a weekender in Berrara, and my friend Bill came to stay with us. Bill was half an hour older than me, and we were born in the same hospital although our mothers never knew each other. Bill and I spent countless hours in the camping ground that was even then imperceptibly changing into a caravan park. It was our base, it was our home, it was where our activities emanated.

Bill and I provided the seafood gourmet meals that the family always enjoyed. My father particularly enjoyed our activities as the food bills were virtually eliminated. We had a boat, a heavy twelve-foot timber-planked skiff made heavier by the fact my father decided to cloak it with fibreglass. Bill and I pulled the boat on the trailer to the creek. We positioned the boat at right angles to the current, and threw out anchors back and front. We let crumbs of bread float down the creek to hungry mullet and garfish looking for food. We obliged by throwing out lines, no sinkers, with cotton wool attached to hooks. We always caught many fish. Mum made the smaller fish into fish cakes, the rest I cooked on the barbeque.

Mullet wasn't the only the staple. Further down the creek we fished for bream and flathead using worms for bait that we caught ourselves. We crossed the creek to reach the beach. The creek was like a teenager, happy and bubbly one minute, morose and dark the next. The entrance of the creek to the ocean could be a raging torrent or a trickle, but was mostly pleasantly easy to cross provided I didn't mind getting wet.

Berrara Beach was a beautiful curved beach that ended at an outcrop of rocks we called Mermaid Rocks. It was typical of a New South Wales south coast beach, with steep berms in the winter and flat hard sand in the summer. We hunted for worms at the top of the tide. We carried a hessian bag containing stinking fish and a small piece of fresh meat. As the tide rushed in we would immerse the hessian bag in the water. As the wave receded we saw V shapes in the sand, tell-tale signs of the presence of worms. We rushed to the V and put our fresh meat at the apex. The worm attached itself to the meat. I placed my thumb and forefinger gently at the back of the worm's head. As the worm arched the end of its body to pull the meat back into the sand, I squeezed it and pulled it out of the sand. Timing in worming, as in life, is everything. Squeeze and pull too early and the result is fresh air. With fresh bait, we fished for whiting off the beach at the entrance to the creek.

The rock platform was our playground with an abundance of octopus and abalone. With fishing lines, we attached three hooks to the end of a stick. We pushed a white rag through one of the hooks. We combed the rock shelf for holes with underwater rock shelves. Waving the white rag under the rock shelves octopi would grab the rag and be hooked. I dragged the octopus from the water and I put my hand over the top of its head. I put my fingers behind its head and found the slit. I turned the head inside out thus killing it. I was careful not to let the octopus get on top of my hands as where their tentacles meet there was a very powerful beak. The most uncomfortable part was the octopus tentacles climbing my arm while it was dying.

My mother cooked octopus and abalone, which we prised from the rocks with our fishing knives. Cunjevoi, a plant-like growth on the rocks, when cut apart produced a meat-like substance that we used to catch rock cod. Further away on Swan Lake Beach we dug our feet in the sand and fossicked for pippies on the run-out tide. We prawned at night with our lamps and hand nets and invariably provided an entrée for the main meal.

Over time Berrara changed. Berrara Road become impassable as a bitumen road was built to connect Berrara to Sussex Inlet. That increased the numbers of both tourists and permanent residents, particularly when electricity and then water came to the area. Over the decades the octopus, mullet, pippies, abalone, worms, prawns and rock cod all but disappeared.

The camping ground changed to a caravan park. The original owner of the camping ground, Gus Kirpson, died and the property was bequeathed to his son Gus. Young Gus was friendly and personable, artistic and well educated. He was not suited to, nor was he interested in, running a caravan park. Trees were the dominant feature of the caravan park. This necessitated winding roads and cul-de-sacs within the park to accommodate the trees. Gus was not interested in the scorched earth, minimum site sizes and precise rectangular blocks of most caravan parks. He liked it the way it was, as did I.

When I bought Berrara Beach Caravan Park from Gus in 1983 it was very neglected. The property's magnificent natural beauty was masked by lantana, overgrown vegetation, neglected amenity blocks and, worst off all, a dumping ground for old buses and rust-ridden eyesores masquerading as caravans. I immediately gave beautiful Berrara the clean-up it needed.

Within two years Josie's sister Dianne and husband Luke managed the caravan park. Their four children were born and raised there. Our frequent visits meant our children became great friends with their cousins. Berrara was the spiritual basis on which unbreakable family relationships were forged. At the heart of this beautiful place was the caravan park.

When I saw those derelict caravans, somewhere in Paris, positioned higgledy-piggedly in the cul-de-sac, I perceived beauty. I remembered Berrara with its winding roads punctuated with trees and the caravans.

The three of us approached one of the caravans. The door opened, and a man who looked to be in his sixties stepped out.

"Bonjour," I said.

He replied in a language I didn't understand.

We were totally unable to communicate except that the handshake was warm and his smile friendly. Brenda quickly told me he wasn't her father.

Brenda ushered me into the caravan. It was late in the afternoon and very gloomy. Brenda said there was no light in the caravan. I sat on a bench seat at the rear, adjacent to the door. Brenda sat on the far side of the caravan on the same bench with her daughter. Her sister sat behind the table near the bench. Opposite the door was a large Mediterranean-looking woman. I had difficulty discerning what she looked like or what she was wearing. At the far end of the caravan, in the gloom, I saw four young children lying on the bed. The conversation was very slow and tedious. The most commonly used words were "comprenez vous?"

Little by little I learnt about Brenda's family, or her version of her family. Her mother was fifty-eight years old. In response to a question from Brenda I disclosed I was sixty-six years old. Brenda introduced me to each of the children lying on the bed. They were her brother's children; he lived in Romania.

There were no men in the caravan, only women and children. Brenda explained that she and her mother and five children plus her baby lived in the caravan. This strained my credulity.

Brenda asked if I want something to eat. I declined.

"When can we get food out of the garbage bins?" I asked.

Brenda's sister, who had not said a word, raised her voice and sharply corrected me. I could sense the hostility. There was a difference between scavenging for food out of garbage bins, and going to the markets to forage for edible food left over at the end of a day's trading. Even at this level of poverty, there was a degree of pride and a social pecking order.

"We cannot go the markets today because they are closed," Brenda stated.

The whole purpose of my visit was thwarted. Brenda was not embarrassed or apologetic. It was just a fact of life.

I was about to learn why the sisters had brought me to the caravan. Little by little, *comprenez vous* by *comprenez vous*, I understood the family was about to be evicted. They had to pay two hundred euros rent the next day.

I was suspicious that Brenda might be entitled to French social security payments.

"I don't know who you are," I said. "I need to see your identity papers."

"No, this is a matter of trust. You have to trust me."

I agreed, sort of, that the issue was trust. "You will not show me your papers, so you don't trust me— why should I give you money?"

The conversation moved back and forth. The word "confiance" (trust) was repeated and there was a Mexican standoff. Suddenly Brenda's mother, who didn't speak French, said something, I presume in Romanian. Brenda agreed to show me her identification papers.

We moved outside the caravan and I looked at her papers under a streetlight. Her name was indecipherable and it wasn't Brenda—she just used that name because it was easy.

When we returned to the caravan, Brenda's mother made me a cup of coffee. A strong brew I enjoyed enormously. I said that I couldn't pay them because I didn't know whether they really owed the money. Brenda's sister volunteered that I could pay the owner direct but I said I had no way of knowing if the so-called owner did, in fact, own the caravan. Brenda and

I agreed to meet at Gare du Nord the next Wednesday to talk about it. The four children lying on the bed were absolutely silent the whole one and a half hours I was there.

Brenda and her sister walked me back to the bus stop. When we arrived Brenda reminded me that I needed to pay her twenty euros. I gave it to her. Brenda was freezing cold, shivering. They waited with me for ten minutes until the bus arrived. Brenda said the bus would take me to Pierrefitte - Stains and told the bus driver where I had to alight. We said au revoir and waved goodbye to each other.

I sat in the bus as it rattled its way to Pierrefitte - Stains. I was disturbed. I laid my head against the window. The thought of them being evicted from their home troubled me. Losing the safety and security of a home was traumatic, something I knew from bitter personal experience. I suddenly felt a sense of loss. I remembered I had only survived due to the kindness of friends. I had places to go, friends to help me, skills and opportunities to rebuild my life but what did Brenda have? What was her future? What was to become of her baby? She was poor, a gypsy, a woman, discriminated against on every level, a victim of society. I thought about her and I felt guilty—I wanted to do something for her, but I didn't. I was racked with sadness and confusion. I dozed off with a picture of her standing on the footpath, shivering.

Eighteen

M. Rogove was my Philosophy Generale tutor. He spoke softly and very quickly, in what I think was French. I would have been no wiser if I had been deaf and unable to lipread.

After Greg's recovery, I sent M. Rogove an email asking for a bibliography. He advised that I needed to read Aristotle's *Metaphysics, Libre A*. The book was difficult, and time-consuming to read, so I abandoned my customary habit of summarising texts. I wasn't particularly worried as I felt I did have some understanding of the text. I had settled into a routine of attending lectures and tutorials, going to the gym and restaurants, and enjoying the odd social contact with Romain. I was oblivious to my actual level of cognition and performance as I had no basis on which to benchmark my progress.

Towards the end of October M. Rogove announced that he wanted to test the students' level of understanding of the course. He wrote two questions on the whiteboard.

1. Quelles sont les causes aristotéliciennes? Donner des exemples.

2. Donner au moins un des argument que donne Aristote contre la théorie platonicienne des Idées.

I didn't know causes existed. I didn't know Plato had any ideas. There was absolutely nothing I could write. I was devastated. I hadn't missed a lecture or a tutorial and yet I didn't have a shred of knowledge to answer the questions written on the board. I had never been in this position before. Even when I scored ten percent for Latin in my Intermediate Certificate exam, at least I knew something.

As I sat slumped in my chair a wave of despair washed over me. I pondered my situation. I could sit in the room and look like an idiot as I folded my arms and wrote nothing, or I could write something. Looking like an idiot was not an attractive proposition. I studied Plato in Art so I wrote about Plato and mimesis, which had little to do with the questions. At least it appeared to the other students and M. Rogove that I knew something. At the end of the tutorial I handed my written paper to M. Rogove, and gave him an embarrassed smile. I knew the little I had written was absolute crappe.

That night I read Aristotle's *Metaphysics A* to understand the causes. I found the passage in the book relating to causes and read it. I couldn't understand it. I then did the unthinkable. I typed the passage from the book into Google translate, and read it.

> *Now the causes are on one quarter. In a sense, by reason we mean the formal substance, or quidite (in fact the reason for being of a thing is reduced definitively to the notion of this thing, and the reason of being primordial is cause and principle); in another sense, the cause is the matter or substrate; in a third sense, it is the principle of movement; in a fourth, which opposes the third, the cause is why, or good (because good is the end of any generation of any movement).*

I couldn't understand the four causes written in English. I had no hope of understanding the four causes in French, let alone writing about them.

Why was I studying philosophy at the Sorbonne? Was it my choice? Whether I actually had a choice was, to me, a huge philosophical issue. I didn't have a choice. Everything I was born with, my every experience, dictated what I did next, thus choice was illusory. The myth of free will was an established philosophical doctrine. I didn't believe it. I also never willingly accepted fate or destiny, although sometimes my mental state severely compromised my ability to make wise choices. Philosophy was a hindrance, not a help, in understanding who I was, or how and why I behaved in a particular way. I was attracted to the philosophical notion that I didn't have a choice because I could avoid responsibility for my predicament. In my heart, I knew I had made a choice to study at the Sorbonne, for which I bore responsibility. It was my hole, my doing.

I sat in my room alone, very homesick. I missed getting up in the morning, wandering up to Mim's for breakfast, having dinner with Josie and our friends, cooking in our new kitchen, and seeing my grandchildren every day. I felt a weight on my shoulders, a darkness and hopelessness; a feeling of being useless and a failure, a loser.

Depression's best friend was mania. I suddenly understood the excitement of coming to Paris, the change of life, the new university and my arrogant faith in my ability to be manic behaviour. I lived in a bubble of my own hubris. The harsh reality was that my language skills were poor, I was struggling academically, and my arrogance had just blown up in my face. I was ashamed and embarrassed by what I had submitted to M. Rogove, the teacher who had made an effort to help me.

I didn't think I was clinically depressed. I had suffered from depression off and on for fifteen years. From one perspective, to be depressed was to be happy. When I was depressed I moved to a state of total isolation, a blackness where no one could hurt me, no one could touch me. I had no worries regarding family, work or financial responsibilities. I withdrew from life; emotional contact or any meaningful connection with anyone was impossible. Life could go on around me, without me. I was untouchable—because I was worthless.

My children were adults. I provided no income for the family. If I died tomorrow everyone would be financially better off because I wouldn't be spending money. What contribution did I make to anyone's life? What was the point of living? I cared for nothing and no one cared about me. I lived in a state of constant emptiness; I had no enjoyment of life as life had nothing for me—yet I was free because the ultimate freedom is the freedom to take your own life. Unfortunately my last attempt, if indeed, it was attempted suicide, was so incompetent as to be derisory. I was driving my Porsche towards Miranda Fair, thinking about my useless pathetic life, when I saw a car parked about fifty metres ahead. I deliberately drove into the back of the parked car, so slowly I didn't even set off the airbags. I left all my details on the car's windscreen and called a tow truck.

Yet within my isolation and blackness I saw things that were normally, to me, invisible. When I got depressed I drove to Berrara, my caravan park, and stayed in a cabin alone. There was no loneliness there; loneliness only existed when I wanted to engage with people. I walked down Berrara Road and knew if I had a gun it would be a short walk. I looked around at the trees—no, I *saw* trees, the different leaves, the different types, shapes, I saw them individually. I observed the sticks on the ground, the odd shapes, the weathered colours, the way that they related to each other, one resting on the other. Normally I looked at things but I didn't see them. In my depression I saw and understood nature, I understood the roots of my creation and my desire to return to the earth.

I cut through the bush and headed for the beach towards Sussex Inlet for breakfast. It was a long walk and the sand was very soft, but time meant nothing. I felt the sun on my cheeks, the wind in my hair. I noticed the waves, different shapes, rolling in at different times with varying power and intensity.

Sussex Inlet was a small village that relied on tourists for much of its prosperity. Even though I had owned Berrara Beach Caravan Park for over thirty years and visited Sussex regularly for over fifty years I was not a local. The best coffee shop in Sussex was closed, so I sat at an outside table at a coffee shop in the heart of the village.

The owner was conducting coarse banter with a local and I was ignored while she exchanged friendly greetings with others, obviously locals. She was a middle-aged woman wearing a loose fitting un-ironed orange blouse over darkish coloured slacks. She had a lined face, was not wearing makeup and her neck showed signs of ageing. The sound of her voice, her choice of words and their intonation filled the air like a fart in a crowded bus.

She finally reached me and said, "Whatduwan?" I ordered omelette on toast with coffee. I noticed that locals arriving after me were served before me. The hostess of this fine dining establishment arrived, and without saying a word, dumped something in front of me, which I surmised was the omelette with two pieces of burnt toast slathered with butter. I could understand her silence—"Mauvais appetite" doesn't have quite the same ring as "bon appetite".

I keenly observed but didn't care. Without the complication of emotion, things became so clear that I saw the world how it truly was; I wasn't clouded with the distraction of personal slights. The irony was that I was happy when I felt like that. The natural world became such an amazing place where life and death were just facts, not issues clouded with emotion or meaning. In the early stages of depression, I could mentally debate with myself the value of life and existence.

Sisyphus was condemned to roll a rock up a hill only to have it roll back down again. Camus likened this to life: we went to work, we came home from work, we went to work, thus life consisted of endless pointless repetition. Camus found value in the repetition itself, that is, the act of pushing the rock up the hill had value and worth in itself. This was life, and when I was depressed I saw little value in anything, let alone trying to understand what possible value there could be in pushing a rock up a hill. As I got more depressed all I wanted to do was sleep under the rock. Sitting in the café, I was under the rock and could only contemplate the appalling service with a sense of resigned detachment. It was not that I didn't care, it was more that I was unable to care. I had a very keen awareness of the service and the type of food presented but I accepted the situation with equanimity and neither rancour nor annoyance. I wasn't unhappy because the sense of detachment and disengagement freed me from life.

Was the depression such that it deprived me of choice? I sank into a state of worthlessness that totally deprived me of the ability to make any judgement about anything. In a state of depression, I had absolutely no rational ability to assess my self-worth, my contribution to those around me, and whether or not it was worth it to me or anyone else that I continued to exist.

The strange thing was that I was still able to function when depressed albeit at a lower level than when I was well. My level of functionality was particularly affected when emotion was required as part of an action. I played sport at a lower level when I was depressed, not because of the reduction in skill level, but because of the absence of the need (not the ability) to concentrate. I lacked the desire to win, the pleasure in the game, and all other emotional attributes essential to playing well. I understood I had responsibilities but my concept of responsibility could dramatically change; what I perceived I was responsible for when I was well disappeared when I was ill. The most significant emotion that affected my ability to function was motivation. When I was completely demotivated achieving anything was difficult. I overcame this when there were things I was required to do, usually particular responsibilities that I couldn't escape.

I sat in my bedroom gloomily considering my situation. I slowly recovered to the point where I thought I should discuss my situation with Damien. I knew Damien was interested in, and had studied philosophy. Shortly after I arrived he gave me one of his textbooks.

Damien was watching television and I asked if I could speak to him. He switched off the TV. I showed him the book, Aristotle's *Metaphysics* A, and told him about the exam. I asked him how I could get on top of my studies. How do I study?

He was very helpful. "You know a philosophy course at the Sorbonne is very difficult."

"Yes, I know. I have just failed an exam. Luckily it doesn't count."

"Philosophy is very difficult even for French students. All French students study philosophy at school so they have a good background before they even get to university."

"I have only done one philosophy subject at Sydney Uni, and it is nothing like philosophy at the Sorbonne. What can I do?"

Damien reached for the TV remote. "The course is far too difficult for you. You cannot possibly pass. I suggest you use your time in Paris to have a good holiday," he said as he dismissed me like a naughty child asking for a lolly.

"Thanks for nothing. I *will* pass, you'll see."

My response to Damien was sheer bravado, an instinctive response to his unhelpful response. I should have known better than to ask him, yet in my heart of hearts I knew he was right. I sat on my bed, miserable and alone, with a decision to make.

I knew I was mentally and emotionally struggling, and yet I was conscious of my personal philosophy; that anyone who had never failed had never achieved anything, and that I learnt far more from my failures and mistakes than my successes. I suffered from low self-esteem and had the continual need to prove to the world that I was successful. If I gave up my studies, I would suffer shame, humiliation and embarrassment. And yet I knew where the road to pushing myself too hard would lead.

As I sat in my room in Damien's flat I considered the consequences of stress, lack of sleep and over-exercise. I was faced with Hobson's choice—give up and suffer the mental and emotional consequences of failure and defeat, or continue and risk a total breakdown. I had been down both roads before—the mortgagee sale of my house and my total collapse when I worked at Pel-Air—neither was pretty. I put my head in my hands, sitting on the edge of the bed. I was desolate. My mind drifted back in time. As I lay on my bed I remembered when I had lost everything, and yet had lost nothing.

I was sitting in my office in Hurstville, after the mortagee sale of my home, when my secretary appeared at the door.

"Hey Russell, there are some guys downstairs who reckon

they're from the sheriff's office, they're going to sell our furniture," she said, quite nonchalantly. She wasn't surprised, the world knew I was in financial trouble.

"Where will I sit?" she asked.

"You can work standing up Scroges, it'll be good exercise." I always called her 'Scroges'—her surname was Scrogie.

We both laughed as I hurried downstairs.

By the time I reached the ground floor they were gone, but not before talking to one of my partners and telling him they would seize the assets of the law firm to pay one of my debts.

A partners meeting was immediately called.

"What's this about, Russell?" Steve asked.

"I don't know. I have got a few judgements against me, and I suppose they think they can put pressure on the legal practice to pay my debts."

"If they take the firm's assets, the firm will collapse," Sharon said.

All my partners were very concerned. I had four partners and we employed over twenty people. It was very difficult, the questions drifted back and forth, but no one was prepared to deal with the elephant in the room. Should I leave the firm? My partners were in no position to demand I leave. They knew it and I knew it. If I left, any access to immediate cash ceased and I needed to live. The firm wasn't travelling well, and we couldn't take out much money, but at least I was getting some money.

"I doubt that anyone can sell the furniture. I always find a way," I said. "I'll sort something out." Intellectually, I absolutely knew where my own interests lay.

I sat back in my chair and I saw the sadness and worry that enveloped my partners. They were pawns in my battle with finance companies. I needed the firm, it was my second family. Every morning when I arrived at work, I walked around the office and said "hello" to every single employee and partner. I thought about my partners, the staff I cared about—emotionally, I didn't have a choice.

"I will leave the partnership, immediately. We can't take a risk. Steve, could you ring the sheriff's office and tell them there is nothing here they can take?" I said, to the palpable relief of everyone in the room.

I was gone within a week. My partners gave me a computer and basic stationery, nothing else. I kept my clients, which didn't affect the firm because no one else could do the aviation work I specialised in. I started to practise from a bedroom in my home. I had computer and typing skills, so I was both solicitor and secretary. Josie went to technical college and learnt Word Perfect so she could do secretarial work. Josie did all the bookkeeping, record keeping, filing, banking and stationery purchases—I concentrated on doing the legal work.

We had no house, my car had been repossessed, I had lost the legal practice, had no income, but worse still it was the cause of my ensuing depression. I had never suffered depression in my life. After these disasters, depression and shingles arrived like a thief in the night. No house, car, income, depressed, self-esteem shattered, but not all was lost.

A beam of light in a dark night was always bright. My days were dark but the lights were very bright. Ross, knowing I was broke and practising from home, gave me ten thousand dollars. It took me years to pay him back. Friends stuck by us, new friends looked after Josie at school, my existing clients supported me. I started to earn a living. My home practice soon became successful. I handed back the car lent to me by a local car dealer, and started to negotiate repayment of my debts, until I was eventually financially secure. I had lost but

I kept, even though I didn't deserve to, the most important thing in the world—my family and true friends.

I sat on my bed, thinking of years before, when I had nothing and yet had everything. I subconsciously knew that no matter how bad things were, they always got better. I remembered the words of Dr. Sonia Wilson, my lecturer at Sydney Uni: "Learning a language is accretive." An epiphany wouldn't convert me to being a French-speaking native; language competence would come gradually, day by day, week by week, month by month. While I was devastated by my failure in M. Rogove's exam, I believed that in other areas of study I was gradually understanding more. I decided to continue. I resolved to work longer hours, not worry about results as they would, for better or worse, take care of themselves, and keep a check on my emotional and mental wellbeing. Within limits, it was essential I maintained a semblance of life outside university; continue to see Brenda, exercise at the gym, and maintain my regular visits to bar/restaurants—the major source of my social activities. I needed routine and normality.

In a perverse kind of way, the whole experience was positive. Any expectation I had of distinctions disappeared, passing any subject would be a bonus, so I temporarily reset my expectations, recalibrated my study habits and decided to press on. I put my situation in perspective; if I failed exams, so what? It didn't compare to losing all material possessions and my self-respect. Emotionally I was a mess, depressed and sad, but intellectually I was still functioning. I am sure there was a philosophical basis by which I could analyse how my mind, body and emotions interacted, but my philosophical analytical ability was so poor, I was totally incapable of undertaking such analysis.

Nineteen

Two days after the exam debacle, Mme Blanc-Benon announced there would be an examination the next week. We needed to be familiar with the books *Aristote Poetique* and *Platon's Republique*. Just what I needed, an exam—not. She also required a dissertation on *Le Modele* due in four weeks.

I was a visual learner. I spent over eight years in full-time study at two universities and my method was always the same. I didn't make any attempt to understand the lecturers. I took copious notes which I then summarised after the lecture. I summarised the summaries close to examination. I did all the required reading (this is a bit of an exaggeration as I failed Accounting 1 and Geography 1 at Sydney Uni) and summarised the texts. I had difficulty learning by listening, as I lost concentration and didn't absorb much. At the Sorbonne, I had access to required reading and subject to my language difficulties and the sheer time it took to summarise the texts I was able to some extent to follow my usual study pattern. I couldn't take notes in lectures. My understanding was so limited, the subject matter so technical, taking notes in lectures was pointless. So I listened and tried to learn. From a learning perspective it was extremely limited, however it obviously helped me absorb the French language itself. I knew if I could access lecture notes I would be much more likely to pass.

One particular woman in the class was very friendly. She always waved to me in the corridor and said *bonjour* when she saw me. She sat in front of me and from time to time helped me. I was tempted to ask for her notes. I was too embarrassed to ask for notes as I felt they were personal. I was afraid she would be embarrassed too. Well, actually that's not right— the real reason I couldn't bring myself to ask for notes was because I had low self-esteem and couldn't cope with the prospect of rejection. I was still depressed, although not as badly as the previous week. I rationalised my decision not to ask for lecture notes on the basis that I was being examined on two books that I had read and understood.

I walked into the exam room in early November. Unusually, for the Sorbonne, I knew what I was to be examined on. The exam consisted of sixteen questions, the first six based on the lectures. Trying to answer those questions was a lost cause. The next ten questions were based on the book Aristotle's *Poetics* and involved commenting on a few sentences from the book. I didn't have the skills to answer with that degree of specificity. I knew I would fail.

After the exam, I sent an email to Mme Blanc-Benon setting out my plight.

I am the oldest foreign student enrolled in your philosophy of art course. Unfortunately I do understand particular information. For example I thought the exam covered the book Aristotle's Poetics *and not Plato. I thought the questions would pose the problem as a longer dissertation. I did not know that there would be questions of the course. If I had known, I would ask a student to give me notes. But it's too late now, it's life!* (Google translation)

She responded:

You are not the only one in this situation and I understand the difficulties of your course in a foreign language. First of all, it is imperative that you take intensive courses of French as a Foreign Language in order to meet the requirements of the Bachelor of Philosophy. The year passes very quickly …
Best regards,
Laure Blanc-Benon (Google translation)

It was a harsh but accurate assessment of my linguistic ability. I was downcast but, having decided to persevere with my studies, I accepted Mme Blanc-Benon's assessment with a degree of equanimity. Mme Blanc-Benon's email provided me with a solution to my study issues so I felt there was a way forward.

The next day I climbed the forty stairs to the top floor of the university and spoke to a secretary in the administration office. The secretary didn't speak English.

"Mme Blanc-Benon says my French is very bad and I need a tutor for my studies. Can you help me?"

"We have tutors that are students who can help."

I had deliberately missed the point of Mme Blanc-Benon's email. My inherent bias against Alliance Francaise meant I still didn't consider an intensive French language course. Mme Blanc-Benon's email rang alarm bells but unfortunately I responded to the wrong alarm; she was suggesting an intensive language course, I thought I needed a tutor.

The secretary gave me the name and email address of a university tutor. After much toing and froing on email with Nicolai, we agreed that he would tutor me for four hours a week. He lived in the sixteenth arrondissement so we agreed to meet at Rue des Ecoles St. Germaine near the old

Sorbonne University. St. Germaine had the benefit of being inconvenient for both of us. I would have two two-hour sessions a week in a local café and we negotiated a rate of thirty euros an hour.

I met Nicolai at St. Michel for the initial tutoring session. Nicolai was not a teacher but a student doing advanced studies at the Sorbonne. He was young, although to me everyone was young. My immediate problem was an essay due in art on the subject of Le Modele in a couple of weeks.

I started to explain the help I needed in writing about Le Modele, when he interrupted.

"I can't help you," he said. "I don't know anything about art."

That was a bit of a setback as I was hoping that he would guide me in this subject. Despite this disappointment, Nicolai was able to help me with every other subject.

Over the next couple of months we met regularly. I was not fussed about the cost. I was not paying Chris Penfold for personal training, so my actual outgoings had decreased since I arrived in Paris.

It was unusual to have private tutoring in cafés. Nicolai enjoyed our café tutoring sessions. On my part cafés were my natural habitat. I was no different from other businessmen. Some of my most difficult and successful negotiations had occurred over lunch in a restaurant. My sessions with Nicolai, in common with my business lunches, were alcohol-free. In my initial email to Nicolai I made it clear the purpose of his tutoring was to help me to pass exams. Nicolai was not entirely reliable. From time to time he changed the time, once he slept in. One time he was immobilised by a soccer injury. As Nicolai could barely walk I met him at his apartment in Rue St. Didier in the sixteenth arrondissement. I walked, Nicolai painfully hobbled to a nearby café.

Over time the benefits of spending four hours a week with Nicolai speaking and listening to French were obvious. Even more importantly it was the vocabulary of the university, of philosophy.

Three weeks after our initial session I wrote a technical essay as part of History and Philosophy of Science. It was about Poincare's text that suggested that even if scientific theories proved to be false there were underlying universal truths. Nicolai suggested I delete one paragraph, but otherwise said the essay was fine.

Nicolai and I discussed Aristotle, Hume and Kant for Philosophie Generale. Nicolai was familiar with philosophers relevant to the subject of the Republique. We didn't discuss philosophers relating to art such as Hegel and Descarte. I passed the essay on Poincare's text; the subject matter was easy—regurgitate the text and give straightforward analysis. The essay on Le Modele was a different kettle of fish.

Twenty

I walked from Damien's apartment to Gare du Nord. It was quite close to Gare de L'Est and was the main hub for inter-suburban trains. I was meeting Brenda but I was not sure if she would be there. I didn't know her mobile number and she didn't know mine. I assumed Brenda had chosen this venue for her own convenience. She didn't know where I lived when she nominated it.

The place suited me, as did the time of one p.m. I studied in the morning, met Brenda and then went to afternoon lectures. I had prepared for our time together. I had no credit cards and only fifty euros in cash. She arrived in her uniform; blue jumper, long dress and purple boots.

There was a narrow street that ran past the exit to Gare du Nord on which there were the ubiquitous bar restaurants. Brenda led me to one that had a small number of outside tables. Brenda was obviously cold; she was shivering but wanted to sit at an outside table. She sat down, opened a packet of cigarettes and proceeded to smoke. She was indifferent to my asthma. She sat quite close to me blowing smoke in my face. I noticed her teeth, stained yellow with nicotine. Her daughter sat restlessly on her lap. Brenda turned her face to avoid blowing smoke in her daughter's face.

She ordered a caffé, I did the same. I lounged back in my chair and lifted the coffee cup to my lips.

"Are you interested in my mother?" she said.

I was astonished by the question. I didn't reflect on why I was so taken aback. I thought if I reflected on my inner thoughts and prejudices, they would reflect badly on me. I parked self-reflection in my subconscious.

"No, of course not!"

"My mother is a putain."

"What is a putain?"

"Someone who sleeps with men."

I explained to Brenda that I had a wife, children and grandchildren in Australia. I confided to her that seeing her and her daughter reminded me of my family in Australia. Carrying her daughter reminded me of my grandchildren. Having Skype and telephone contact didn't substitute immediate close personal contact. Skype projected images, but it masked feelings, obscured body language and only dulled the pain of separation created by distance.

Brenda confessed that she didn't have a baby. The baby she referred to when I first met her on the street was her sister's baby.

Then her voice became venomous and she was very emotional. "I would rather sleep on the street with my child than live with my mother."

My immediate thought was that we wouldn't be discussing buying or renting a caravan. I could now relax; any guilt I might have felt in that regard evaporated.

Over the next hour, with my painfully bad French and repeated "je ne comprend pas" I began to understand the problem. Brenda and her toddler lived in the caravan with her mother. The other four children appeared to have found alternate accommodation, or more likely were brought into the caravan for the occasion in order to assist in Brenda's attempt to emotionally blackmail me into buying her a caravan.

Her toddler daughter was always crying and her mother was angry with the child for crying. The toddler's distress caused conflict between Brenda and her mother. I was not in the least surprised. Brenda's mother was fifty-eight years old. It would be very difficult to live in such close and cramped quarters with a two-year-old. Not having lights in the caravan could only exacerbate the situation. It would be a nightmare for a woman of her age.

I tried to explain this to Brenda.

"It must be very difficult for your mother. When you're old you lose patience."

Brenda's reply was swift and derisory.

"She is a putain!"

I watched Brenda's daughter wriggle restlessly on her lap and knew further discussion was pointless. As I sat talking to Brenda, I felt calm and relaxed, my own difficulties and struggles evaporated. Being with Brenda and her daughter, and understanding her difficulties, discussing the problems somehow gave me a sense of security, a connection to my family back home. I couldn't help her, any advice I gave her was ignored, yet I felt her anger, her distress and her bond with her daughter. I was remote from her and her life, but at this moment I wasn't, I was part of her life.

I changed the subject. I wanted to understand gaspillage. I asked her to take me to the markets so I could see how she foraged for food. She agreed to take me to the markets on Sunday. We were to meet at Gare St. Denis.

It was time for me to go. I got up, walked to the shop next door, and bought Brenda a packet of cigarettes. She didn't ask me to. I also gave her twenty euros, as she expected.

Twenty-one

Five days after the art exam M. Kammerer started the class as usual by marking the roll and posing questions to other students. After half an hour he said, "Now we are going to do the exam and you have one hour." He then wrote the questions on the blackboard. I had no idea there was to be an exam. Nobody had told me.

There were four questions.

The first question was: What is a valid argument?

I knew the answer to this. An example of a valid argument is, if all wives are good cooks and my wife is married (presumably to me) she is a good cook. That is a valid argument. It can't be wrong as a matter of logic.

The second question was to give two examples of inductive reasoning that give contradictory conclusions. I knew this because we have Ingham's chickens in Australia.

While Bertrand Russell never knew the Ingham chicken farms, he provided an excellent example of inductive reasoning that converted exactly to the experience of the chickens on Ingham chicken farms. You could imagine the Inghams on their chicken farm feeding their chickens every day.

The chickens in cages were fed daily, kept out of the weather and in a warm environment. The chickens were happy even if their accommodation was a bit cramped.

The chickens said to each other, "Mr. Ingham comes to feed us every day, he is a nice kind man."

One chicken flaps and cackles, "How do you know he is a nice man?"

"Because he feeds us every day! Now shut up you idiot."

Then one day Mr. Ingham gave the chickens a lot more feed. The chickens thought Mr. Ingham was absolutely wonderful, except for the maverick chicken that was suspicious. A week later Mr. Ingham came and wrung the chickens' necks.

The fact that Mr. Ingham fed the chickens every day could mean that he was either a very nice man, or he was fattening them up to kill them. The two outcomes are contradictory.

Inductive reasoning was the very basis on which we lived our life. While inductive reasoning was used in science to create a hypothesis, it was discussed by Hume, Kant and other philosophers in the context of experience. The sun rose every day, so inductively or by experience we postulated that the sun would rise tomorrow and so we acted accordingly.

The other two questions related to Goodman's paradox, the Hempel's paradox and Popper's refutability. I handed in the exam paper confident I had passed. I asked M. Kammerer what notice we were given. He explained that he told us in class the previous week. I said I didn't understand what he said. He looked at me sympathetically and said nothing. There was nothing he or I could do. It didn't matter, I thought. I would pass anyway.

The next week M. Kammerer handed back the results and gave me a mark of thirty-five percent. I understood the questions, I knew the answers and I had no idea why M. Kammerer gave me such a low mark. I was not discouraged by the low mark, I accepted it and moved on with my studies. My mental and emotional state had improved somewhat and I had become more confident that I was acquiring knowledge and my understanding had improved. I had commenced private lessons with Nicolai and felt less isolated and believed I would quickly close the gap between failure and success.

I continued to inhabit the library most days of the week. I always passed the woman on the street, ignoring her receptacle for money, although we always exchanged bonjours. After Kammerer's exam, in which I thought I did rather well, and felt happy rather than depressed, I asked her what she wanted.

"Nettoyage," she said, which was French for cleaning. Twenty metres from where she usually sat was the Intermarché Express. This was a general store the equivalent of an IGA store in Sydney. She put the toddler in the pram and left it at the entrance to the supermarket.

Suddenly a young man appeared carrying a shopping basket. I didn't mind, but I surmised that he was obviously watching and she had somehow signalled him. The first two items she chose were hair shampoo and nappies. She then grabbed a can of baked beans (she wanted more but I controlled what she bought), onions and cleaning products. The total was forty-eight euros, more than half being the cost of nappies. At the checkout counter the woman serving had a face like stone. I have rarely seen such an unfriendly, unwelcoming face and never, ever in a supermarket.

When we emerged from the supermarket I was immediately surrounded by about four other people I assumed were family members. One old woman, a wizened old crow, showed me her mobile phone, and demanded two euros. A middle-aged man, scruffy, ill-kempt with what appeared to be dirty stubble on his face wanted money for coffee. The other two leeches, a man and a woman, jabbered at me. It was a cacophony of sound with each person vying for my attention.

"Non, non!" The words spat out of my mouth.

They continued to harass me with their demands. They encircled me and although I was trapped, I didn't feel threatened or intimidated.

"Fuck off you arseholes," I yelled as I pushed past the old crow into clear air. I marched down the rue towards the library without looking back.

The next day I walked past the woman she accosted me and tried to get me to take her, again, to the supermarket. The following day the same thing happened. Her smile was now very ugly; I could see that she had black broken teeth, dirty hair and was very fat. She was repulsive. I brushed past her, ignoring her for the next few days before she got the message, and stopped harassing me.

A short time later I sat in the bar near my room drinking my morning coffee when I started to think about the woman on the street. I was sitting at the bar beside two middle-aged women. They were friends, well dressed with matching pearl necklaces, who regularly met and had coffee in the morning.

"Is it okay to give money to people on the street?" I asked the barman.

"Definitely not. Those people sitting on the street are Romanians whose business is to collect money. They use babies and children as bait. When they see an idiot arrive they signal each other."

I then knew why the woman in the supermarket was so stony-faced. I didn't begrudge the money I spent; the woman I bought nappies and food for was very poor, and the money meant little to me.

The woman sitting next to me chimed in.

"Don't give them money, but if you see a woman on the

street, give her food, nappies or cleaning wipes. If you give her money it is taken away from her."

I was too embarrassed to tell my barman friend I had already made a significant contribution to the Romanians' (Gites') business. I asked Damien what he thought about me giving money and providing food to the Romanians. "Ca trouve elle a plus d'argent que toi (she's got more money than you)," he said, speaking French for the first time since I arrived.

It wasn't true, but I got the point.

I continued to pass her each day without giving her money. One day I walked past her and walking beside me was a Frenchman in his mid-thirties. I asked him if the woman we passed was Romanian. He spoke very quickly and angrily. I didn't understand what he was saying but I knew the word "voler" meant steal. When I changed the subject, he was very pleasant and we chatted for a few minutes before going our separate ways.

The change in his demeanour was like a ray of sunshine peeping through the clouds after a thunderstorm. I discussed the situation with French women (strangers) in restaurants and with bar persons. Their unanimous view was that I should not give money, but it was quite appropriate to provide food or nappies.

I was struck by what appeared to be blatant racism of the Frenchman in the street. In my time in France I was generally unaware of racism. To the contrary, the French were very tolerant toward the poor and disadvantaged, irrespective of their race. Gypsies, mainly men, were an exception, although compared to the events in Cronulla, the French were a model of tolerance towards gypsies.

I lived in Cronulla for some years before and after the infamous Cronulla riots. For a few years before the riot on December 11, 2005, I walked to Cronulla along the shores of Gunnamatta Bay. As the tide receded I walked from my rented house, continued past the houses jammed together along the foreshore to Gunnamatta Park at the end of the bay. The park was a favourite picnic spot for the Muslim community.

I liked to see Muslim families in the park. Blankets were spread out; old men would smoke pipes; their wives, wearing long dresses and headscarves, sat drinking coffee, watching over young children playing nearby. Three generations often enjoyed Gunnamatta Park.

Cronulla's main parks, Gunnamatta, Oak, Shelly Beach and South Cronulla had communal barbeques and grassy open areas for families to sit and have picnics. These parks were very popular; they were places where families, strangers to each other, shared the grass spaces, communal seats, barbeques, pristine ocean and bay views on balmy Sunday afternoons. The parks were places to congregate, relax and enjoy each other's company.

Cronulla was a beachside suburb, the only beach in Sydney directly accessible by train. The local community was proud of its beaches, parks, and its lifesavers—volunteers who gave up weekends to keep the beaches safe. I joined Cronulla Surf Life Saving Club in my thirties and passed the swimming and resuscitation tests.

Each Sunday I swam with a local magistrate (now called a judge) in the over thirties swimming race. We swam into the ocean, around some buoys anchored offshore and back to the beach. The magistrate was captain of the club and always let everyone else in the field lead him back to the beach. I kept him company.

By 2005 Cronulla had changed. As I walked past Gunnamatta Park, there were very few people who were not obviously Lebanese or Muslim. I regularly ran in Cronulla. The running routes took me through and past the other parks as I ran from my home to Wanda Beach and back. I was aware of the change, but I wasn't particularly concerned. One change that I did notice was that some Muslims appropriated the park for their exclusive use. Muslim families roped off large areas of the park surrounding barbeques to prevent others using part of the park or the barbeques.

At the same time as the Lebanese community was occupying the parks in large numbers, to the exclusion of local people, there was a more dangerous and insidious invasion.

I first became aware of it while running through Oak Park. A number of Lebanese young men were playing football. To protect other users, this is forbidden. A football hit me in the back. A well-muscled young man of Lebanese appearance said, "Sorry mate, but you shouldn't be here, we're playing a game."

"You shouldn't be playing here," I retorted.

This was a foretaste of reality in Cronulla. Groups of young Lebanese men hunted in packs in Cronulla. Young, Anglo Saxon males were their prey. They were like white pointers in a seal colony.

Packs of Lebanese men congregated on what was known as 'The Wall', between Eloura and North Cronulla. They parked their cars, lowered their windows, festooned with ribbons, radios blaring on the edge of the walkway running from Cronulla to Wanda. They were loud, and verbally and physically intimidated passersby. I stopped running to Wanda.

The assaults by these young men were notorious. Always packs against lone strangers. The police were intimidated by the thuggery, were powerless and failed to protect the community. These packs of white pointers had no respect for authority, and no respect for the rights of locals to use the beaches and parks. The community was powerless and angry. I was angry.

Just before the riots, the Cronulla golf club held a function in a building at Gunnamatta Park. Two Lebanese young men were caught stealing alcohol. The alcohol was taken from them and they were sent on their way. Thirty minutes later about thirty Lebanese young men yelling abuse approached the building. The golf club members, mostly elderly, locked themselves inside while the Lebanese men hurled foul epithets and smashed chairs against the building. The police were called. As usual, they arrived well after the Lebanese men left so no arrests were made.

The bonfire was built, fuel was being added and all that was needed was a match. Word of an assault on a young lifesaver spread like wildfire. The shooting of Archduke Ferdinand was the catalyst for the start of World War I, the assault of the lifesaver was the catalyst for the Cronulla riots. Calls went out on social media to take back the beaches.

Over five thousand people converged on Cronulla. The peaceful protest turned into an ugly, hate-filled afternoon of alcohol-fuelled violence. The ugly face of this violence was Troy Dennehy.

There were two well-known 'Nuggets' in the Cronulla surfing community. They were both very good surfers. One was my son Damien, the other Troy Dennehy. Both were known by the nickname Nugget.

Damien and Troy knew each other; they surfed together and competed against each other. They were in the same surf club. The Troy that Damien knew was a boy with a great love for the surf. He was a sad and lonely boy, badly affected by the breakup of his parents' marriage. He grew up in a violent household and had an aggressive personality. Other surfers were wary of him. His expertise was surfing the Alley. The Alley was the surf break near North Cronulla Surf Club where Damien learnt to surf. Troy was the king of the Alley and loved it best when the surf was snarling and angry. Troy won the Alley Masters three times, was Cronulla regional champ and took out the Newcastle Mattara contest. Troy was normally happy, worked as a tradesman and just loved Cronulla and surfing. The other love of his life was his Japanese wife.

As part of the riot, Troy, fueled with alcohol, took part in two mob attacks on defenceless Lebanese-looking men. He jumped on the boot of a police car, and assaulted police and ambulance officers. It was an outpouring of emotion and anger, the like of which his friends had never witnessed before.

Troy handed himself over to the police and was charged with riot and affray. The magistrate gave him bail and he ultimately served a long community service order. Troy was deeply ashamed of his actions and gave a written apology to the Lebanese community.

Troy, personally, bore the shame of the actions of all those who participated in the riots. Whenever a picture of the riots appeared it was invariably of Troy's contorted rage-filled face. Suffering from depression, he was badly affected by the shame and publicity of his actions. He struggled for two years. On the 19th November 2007 Troy, sadly, ended his pain by hanging himself. Cronulla lost a much loved, respected young man.

Where and when racism appeared, in France, confused me. Racism appeared to be related to gypsies, although women in particular, in Paris, were sympathetic to gypsy women. They believed they were exploited. I wondered why racism in Australia was more prevalent than in France. France's national motto was liberte, egalite, fraternite—the French lived by it. People lived in a community, free to do what they liked without harm to others, as equals for the common good. A sense of community transcended the individual. Fraternity was about moral obligation. Australian culture was individual enterprise, the protection of individual civil liberties, the common good far less important. Self-interest transcended moral obligation, as anyone who has dealt with an Australian bank would know. Racism occurred in France when the French motto was trashed. The man on the footpath who railed against gypsies described them as thieves; gypsies acted without regard to others, and attracted condemnation. Australian racism appeared to occur when Australians suffered real or imagined threats to their lifestyle, jobs, or way of life. This represented a threat to individuals. Threats to jobs or lifestyle didn't appear to be an issue in France.

Twenty-two

I had an essay on Le Modele due late November. It constituted part of my final mark for Philosophy of Art. Typical of the Sorbonne I had to write a dissertation on Le Modele. Of course there was no assistance, no guidance. What was certain was that I had to find a paradox. Philosophy at the Sorbonne existed in the realm of paradoxes.

I was an expert in paradoxes, my particular expertise being in the paradox of spending.

I saved money by spending it. This seems absurd and contradictory and, as such, is a paradox. Josie questioned the amount of money I spent on breakfast each day.

"I buy breakfast every morning because it is cheaper than buying lunch, so I save a fortune," I said.

I doubted Mme Blanc-Benon would accept this paradox so I settled for demonstrating that Euclidian geometry and Kant's moral theory were both models deductively valid and at the same time false.

I worked very hard on the dissertation for a week, and sent my draft plan to Mme Blanc-Benon for confirmation that I was on the right track. I didn't expect a problem.

Mme Blanc-Benon replied,

> *Dear sir,*
>
> *Regarding the method of dissertation, I had said in the course of time that I would be indulgent with foreigners, but you still have to learn about the method of dissertation: it is not a question of essay on a theme. It is necessary to address the multiple aspects of the concept of model and you cannot restrict yourself to the ethical model, especially for a philosophy course of art. At least it is necessary to establish a link with the course and the question of mimesis.*
>
> *You can ask for advice from a French student and tutors are there to help you understand the method.*
>
> *You can come and talk to me at the break on Wednesday if you want some more details.*
>
> *Best regards,*
> *Laure Blanc-Benon* (Google translation)

On Wednesday Mme Blanc-Benon took the initiative and asked the class if someone would help me with the dissertation. The friendly woman sitting in front of me immediately volunteered to help. I met with her at the end of the class. She was quite young, had blonde hair draped over her shoulders and wore glasses. She was medium height and build. With her blue eyes and pale skin she looked more English than French. She had a huge smile and an obvious *joie de vivre*. Her friendliness, enthusiasm and love of life shone like a beacon.

She introduced herself as Anne and we swapped email addresses.

I sent Anne an email that set out the plan of my dissertation. Anne wrote back that I had to explain what the paradox was in the model. She added that there was a paradox in almost every concept in philosophy. She gave me an example.

Assume the dissertation is about chocolate. The problem with chocolates is that they are good because you enjoy eating it and bad because it is fattening, addictive and bad for your health. There is a third way. Chocolates are not so bad because they provide moral support that is good for your health. The dissertation argues each case and finally comes to a conclusion.

Anne provided me with what I needed. The rest of her email, written in English, explained:

That's the same thing about the modele because, of course, when you imitate something, you're close to the thing that you're imitating since this is the "modele", but you are also not so close because if it's the same thing, is it still a "modele"?? This is the problem and you are not supposed to give the solution to that in the introduction BUT in the conclusion!

The dissertation is about you thinking by yourself and only using the Philosophers, the artists, or the books to support your different arguments. Of course, most of the time, a philosopher has already said before the argument that you're using. So, it's important to quote him when you use this argument, and to explain precisely what he says (in what book, etc.), but it's only in a middle of YOUR general argumentation, YOUR general reflexion.

Dissertation is kind of typically French because the idea is kind of "Ok so I'm going to take a problem and answer it using all philosophers or all people who said something about it, but in my OWN reflexion", it's maybe kind of pretentious, but that's the exercise though.

I really hope that will help you.

Please if you have any other questions or need anything don't hesitate to ask.

Good luck!
Anne

This was all pretty easy really. All I had to do was outline the paradox, deal with the arguments for and against and find the third way. The arguments had to be supported by reference to various philosophers. The dissertation was to be written in French to a tertiary standard.

I redid the dissertation and had lengthy discussions with Anne via email on the contents of my dissertation. At one point, she expressed concern that she may not be giving me accurate guidance, as she was only a student. I told her the dissertation was my responsibility not hers. Her help ensured that my mark was much better than if I had struggled on my own. My contact with Anne effectively ended my isolation at uni. By this time, I had talked to other students in the corridors, on occasions walked to the station with students and chatted on the platform. The interaction with Nicolai, Anne and other students meant I was more comfortable in my student environment. As my feeling of isolation receded and my language skills improved, my mental outlook stabilised to the point I became positive about my progress.

I spent days rewriting the dissertation and handed in the completed dissertation on the due date.

Relieved that I handed in the assignment, in a momentary lapse of judgement I decided to talk to Damien about my proposed rendezvous with Brenda.

He took my notification of the proposed meeting well.

"You are beyond stupid. You don't listen to anything I say."

"Other than your assertion that I am stupid is there any reason why I shouldn't go to Saint-Denis in broad daylight to meet a young woman and her child?"

"Of course there's a reason. Saint-Denis is a very rough, rundown slum area. It's notorious for robberies. You will be very lucky if you're not bashed and robbed."

I was used to Damien's hyperbole by now.

"So, you won't go to Saint-Denis to meet this woman?"

"Yes, I will."

It was Sunday afternoon and I exited Gare Saint-Denis. I stepped onto a very large open space which reminded me of a concrete apron outside an aircraft hangar. I was no longer in France, I was somewhere in Africa. There were crowds of people overwhelmingly of African appearance. They were of both sexes, all ages, but predominately young men.

Brenda arrived, alone, in uniform. We walked through the crowds towards the bridge crossing the nearby canal. We threaded our way through groups of young African men, laughing, jocularly pushing each other. Others danced, tapped their feet and jiggled their bodies in time to music played through headphones clapped to their ears. Smoke billowed in the air from street vendors burning kebabs. Everyone was having fun, and it was infectious.

I was not uncomfortable. I was with Brenda. Brenda survived on the streets every day so I instinctively knew I was safe. I was vaguely aware of the risk of young African men. There was no reason to be uncomfortable, such vague awareness was no more than my latent racial prejudice. We crossed the canal and veered left down a wide road, sans cars, with four tram tracks down the middle. On either side were narrow footpaths where everyone, without exception, walked. We came to a church, veered right along the side of the church and arrived at another street where we faced a pedestrian mall stretching into the distance.

I felt safe with Brenda despite Damien's warning, but my awareness of being in the midst of young African men, while being devoid of anxiety, reflected my underlying propensity to depression. This underlying depression was masked by my

connection to Nicolai and Anne and a few other students—
I was superficially stable, however depression never left me, it
just took a holiday from time to time. When I was depressed
my risk boundaries dramatically changed which is the reason
I ended up living on the street when I returned to Sydney.
I couldn't comprehend why I needed or wanted to see
Brenda, all I knew was that being with her somehow made
me happy.

We walked down the mall to an outside table at the
restaurant Grappe d'Or. We sat down, ordered coffee, and
Brenda smoked. I surveyed my surroundings and observed
that the mall was very attractive. It was really a long quite
wide street closed to traffic. There were families, people old
and young. Everyone was happy; the atmosphere was like a
carnival. I was relaxed, in another world.

My French conversation class was about to begin. Brenda
was raised in Arad in Romania in a family home that was
now abandoned. The sides of her mouth turned down, her
head hung slightly and she had a faraway look in her eyes.
She wanted to own a house. I felt pangs of sympathy that
soon disappeared as the inevitable attempt to create space
between me and my wallet began.

"My brother is in Romania. He has to pay maintenance
for his children. Unless he pays two thousand euros he will
go to gaol."

"Are those the children I saw in the caravan?"

"Yes."

I absorbed this information and resisted the temptation to
ask further questions.

My wealth had arisen from the unlikely opportunities given
to me after a custody case that my client could never win.
Brenda was not to know that her attempt to elicit sympathy

for her brother switched me into lawyer mode, in which I instinctively rejected any responsibility to help her brother meet his obligations.

I started practice as a solicitor in Hurstville in 1973 for my father who was a sole practitioner. When I first started work there was nothing for me to do. Harry Wanstall, a local solicitor sometimes referred his family law clients to me. These clients either had a hopeless case or were impecunious. Harry was in his sixties, a thin man with a bald head. He would rush into court, his body swinging on the crutch under his left arm. When he reached the bar table, always at the last minute, he would survey his waiting opponents, ceremoniously drop in front of him the files he carried, position his crutch within reach and balance on his only leg. He acted as if he owned the place. I once asked him why he always sent me clients with a hopeless case. Harry, who kept his sense of humour somewhere in the leg that had been amputated years before, said, "I always match the quality of the client's case with the competence of the lawyer."

One day I was sitting in my office busily occupied completing the *Sydney Morning Herald* quick crossword when the phone rang.

"Russell, I have a problem. Can you come to court straight away?"

"What's the problem Harry?" I asked.

"I will tell you when you get here."

I walked into Harry's office to learn of his plight. The procedure at Kogarah court was simple. When a case was to be heard, the court officer called out the names of each party involved in the case. The people whose names were called walked into court and stood behind their solicitor sitting at the bar table.

On the day Harry rang, a case on the list was a custody

dispute over a six-year-old girl Cassie. The court officer called out, "Cheri Fisher, Maria Tallis."

Both women walked into court and stood behind Harry.

Oops. Harry had accepted instructions from two females wanting custody of the same child and, in his dotage, had not realised until they stood behind him.

I tried, unsuccessfully, to hide the smirk on my face as Harry relayed the dilemma. He wanted me to act for one of them.

Cheri Fisher was indigenous, twenty-three years old and Cassie's natural mother. Three years earlier she had left Cassie in Mrs. Tallis's care. Mrs. Tallis was seventy years old and was and had been foster mother to many children. Cheri wanted Cassie back. Mrs. Tallis wanted to keep her.

"Let me guess, Harry. We have two women, one's the young natural mother, and the other is an unrelated old lady with one foot in the grave. I bet you want me to act for the old lady."

"You're very perspicacious, Russell."

And so it was.

My secretary told me that I had an appointment with David Cross, a person with whom I was unfamiliar. David ushered Mrs. Tallis into my office and sat in front of me. He told me he was the general manager of a well-known aviation company. Mid-thirties, he wore an expensive suit and was well spoken. He had an air of confidence and authority.

He asked me what was happening to Cassie. I was really surprised. I then learnt that David was one of Mrs. Tallis's foster children. I advised them that Mrs. Tallis had absolutely no chance of obtaining custody of Cassie. The best thing she could hope for was access. Both wanted custody of Cassie and both wanted Cassie to have nothing to do with the other. It was common ground, but not very helpful.

The discussions with Harry to reach an agreement regarding Cassie were protracted. David wanted to know every detail of our discussions and the progress of negotiations. During the process we became friends. He sold me a new aluminium tinny manufactured by a subsidiary of his company and we started to go fishing in the Georges River.

Six months after we met, David established his own aircraft sales business. I became the company's external solicitor. He later established another business selling Learjets and Saab Fairchild Aircraft. I travelled the world; Paris, London, Linkoping, Tucson, San Antonio, Singapore and Bangkok to negotiate aircraft sales contracts and distributor agreements. I developed an aviation law practice.

The course of opportunity was convoluted; it twisted and wound like a river on a flat plain. Opportunity followed its nose, looked for ways to travel and was usually blind. Opportunity didn't foresee where it would be in the future. My future was to become a director and shareholder of Pel-Air Aviation and a director of a publicly owned airline. I very much doubted that helping Brenda's brother would lead anywhere other than me being considerably poorer. I was totally unable to see any benefit either commercial or personal that could arise from being involved in a custody dispute in Romania.

Brenda wanted to walk. We walked down the pedestrian rue. There were rows of clothing stores punctuated by the odd fast food place, a pharmacy and one or two restaurants. We passed Athletes Foot, Sophie, Jennyfer, Zimo, Princess, Miss Shoes and many others.

We chatted. She again said she wanted a house, security for her daughter. Hopes and dreams were not restricted by wealth, circumstances or present reality. I was rarely present as

I lived in my head. My concept of reality was fantasy. I always lived my life in pursuit of goals and as to smelling the roses, I didn't know there were any roses. I asked myself if Brenda's ambition was fantasy. I hoped not.

We strolled down the rue. I noticed vendors, all Africans, sitting on the ground with white cotton cloths spread in front of them. They sold wallets, handbags, watches, sunglasses, maps and CDs.

"When can we look for food?"

"It is too late," she said. "The markets are closed."

"Why didn't we go before they closed?"

For the first time, we had a conversation I didn't understand. I knew Brenda was obfuscating but I didn't know why. I wasn't sure, but I thought she said that scavenging for food at the markets was not something I should do.

We kept walking and she showed me her boots with large holes in the sole. She walked into a shop selling shoes. She picked out a pair of boots for me to buy. When I said I didn't have any money she said I could use a credit card. I didn't have a credit card to pay the shop owner twenty-five euros to layby the boots. I deliberately left my credit card at home as I was worried Brenda would persuade me to use it.

I felt emotionally vulnerable when I was with Brenda. I was acutely aware of how my children were able to extract money from me; I had difficulty saying no. My children's methods varied from manipulation, presenting me with a need for me to assist, smooth talking, and sometimes a simple request. None of my children's requests were unreasonable, and the reality was that I helped where I could. Mel, for example, declared she was moving out of home to rent a unit. Renting was a waste of money so I helped her buy a one-bedroom unit in Cronulla. She was nineteen years old. My children gave far more to me than I gave to them.

Not so with Brenda. I knew Brenda made a living separating strangers from their money, and I was a sitting duck; sooner or later I would end up giving her a lot of money. I protected myself by emptying my pockets before I saw her, and then when the requests came, I emotionally disconnected. She was only a stranger who met me to extract money. When she asked for the boots, and I refused because I had no money, she accepted my rebuff with equanimity. She always did. Yet something about my dismissal of her obvious need made me uncomfortable, not guilty, just left a nagging disquiet.

Twenty-three

In late November M. Slama announced a voluntary practice test in Philosophie Moderne. I accepted the offer with alacrity. It was one month after my disastrous exam with M. Rogove and I knew that I had improved considerably. My help from Anne, sessions with Nicolai, talking with Brenda, Fahat and locals in bars had borne fruit. I liked studying Descartes and was genuinely interested in his philosophy of "I think, therefore I am".

I walked into the exam room at the appointed time and was handed a sheet of paper by M. Slama. The sheet of paper contained a passage from Descartes and I was required to provide an oral commentary. Typical Sorbonne; there was no help, no guidance, just give a commentary.

I read the text and recognised it immediately. It was from Descartes' first principles and discussed the necessity for doubt in order to reach the truth. I was an expert. I would say to my children, "Where were you last night?" The usual reply conformed with what they thought I wanted to hear. It was only after expressing considerable doubt that the truth surfaced.

I sat in front of M. Slama and had no difficulty dealing with the subject matter. I had studied hard and was very knowledgeable. At the end of my dissertation, I looked at M. Slama and he looked at me. The look on his face told me my dissertation was a disaster. He said nothing but I knew, I felt it. I saw the disappointment, or was it disbelief—how could it have been so bad?

That night I sent an email to M. Slama.

Thank you for the exam today. I do not know if my dissertation was bad or good, but I think that was bad. I hope you understand that I studied diligently. It's important that I learn from experience. I understand that I didn't analyse the text. The text begins with the statement that one must only seek for the truth and we doubt the existence of all. The question is the role of doubt in the search for truth. Because I did not analyse the passage I missed the point. Indeed I used the text as a garbage for my knowledge!

Is it a correct balance over my dissertation? I am not prepared to use the difficulty of languages to excuse bad performance. But maybe the problem is the difficulty of the French method.

What are you thinking? (Google translation)

At 7:30 the next morning M. Slama replied in an email:

Dear Sir,

I thank you for your message. Of course I understand that you need time to get used to our country, its language, its "ways" academic! and I admire your courage to come to the Sorbonne to face the most difficult French texts, which I try as much as I can to make loved.

Your record is perfectly correct. The problem of your oral comes from a question of method: from the text that I gave you to comment, you spoke of quite another thing, especially the "Letter-preface" and notions that were not found not at all in Articles 1, 2 and 3. It would be enough for you to concentrate on the text itself, word after word, sentence after sentence, and to follow precisely Descartes' argumentation. I recommend, at first, to buy an English translation of the Principles of Philosophy.

Here is a copy available online: http://Simson. amazon.com/Principles-Philosophy-Rene-Descartes/dp/ 1604597402

Work the text in the following article by article, helping you in my class, and you will manage to explain it in a very convincing way!

Do not hesitate to write to me if you miss certain points, I will try to answer you as far as possible.

Best regards,

Paul Slama (Google translate)

If failure constituted success I was a gold medal winner in many areas of my life. I translated my failure in studies successfully to the gym. Men were sole users of the area where I exercised in the Parisian gym. In the main, the men exercising were magnificent physical specimens. They had washboard stomachs, huge chests, large carved biceps and legs like tree trunks. I had never attempted bodybuilding but when I first joined the French gym I had decided to start. I copied the exercises done by others. I knew my technique was correct. Chris was a stickler for doing exercises in a particular manner. He contended each exercise had a particular technique and failure to replicate it would result in long-term injury.

Months later my body was unchanged. Why hadn't my body evolved? My skinny arms and legs were the same. I still had the chest of a boy. The only logical explanation was that I had not meticulously copied the actions of the magnificent specimens I admired. I continued my exercises and introduced another routine. It was a routine faithfully followed by every body-builder in the gym. In doing so, I ignored the lessons of Plato.

Plato starts with an idea. The idea is then created as a form and is imitated as a painting. Plato contended the imitation was inferior to the form. A chair was an example. First was the idea of a chair, subsequently the carpenter created the chair. The painter, who made a painting of the chair, created an image. Plato postulated that the image (painting) was inferior to the real thing, the actual chair. I didn't believe Plato—nor did Hegel, although I don't know why. I was studying Hegel in Art but his ideas were too difficult for me to comprehend.

I looked at myself lovingly in the mirror. The look of adoration was the key to success. I put my shoulders back, sucked my breath in and held my chest out. I hunched my shoulders forward and held my arms in an ape-like pose. I bent my elbows, clenched my fists either side of my ears and tightened my biceps. I was gorgeous.

I practised this for a month. It worked: I saw embryonic muscles appear, my chest was larger, my stomach flatter. Every time I saw my body in the mirror it looked better. I was more gorgeous than ever.

There were setbacks: in order to improve my body, I couldn't look at any other male in the gym. I learnt to look, but not see. I became totally unaware of anyone else. I was self-absorbed in the beauty of my own body. I was so successful that staff at the gym gave me special consideration. As I entered the gym someone invariably pointed to the weights.

"Votre chez les dents c'est la," they said, always with a welcoming smile.

It was only after I returned to Australia that I understood what they said; "Your toothpicks are there."

Twenty-four

I was walking out of the lecture room when yet another student who had learnt to speak English over the last couple of months approached me.

"Do you hear Serge say we are having an exam in a couple of weeks?"

I had never heard a French student use the given name of a lecturer before.

When I said I didn't know, he continued, "Yes, he said he is going to give us a text and we have to write a commentary."

I was grateful for his thoughtfulness. I remembered the debacle of my Philosophy of Art assignment on Le Modele and M. Slama's practice exam.

That evening I consulted Damien on an email I proposed to send to M. Audier. I wanted to make sure there were no spelling mistakes or grammatical errors.

Damien, as usual, was very helpful. "You can't send that!"

"Why not?" I said. "Where are the mistakes?"

"Actually, there are no mistakes," he said. "Google translate is quite good, but your email is very disrespectful."

I was genuinely nonplussed by what he was saying.

"You may think you're being funny, but French lecturers do not have a sense of humour—they demand respect."

I searched my email for the signs of disrespect. I read the first paragraph.

I am the old foreign student in your class. I have been told, by other students, that the examination consists of examination of a text and writing a commentary. The only commentary I have previously made is on the quality of my wife's cooking.

I then asked him to explain what he meant by a commentary and what texts I had to read. Damien grabbed my laptop and deleted the offensive sentence. I told Damien I was grateful for his editing as it probably saved me from embarrassment. I took the laptop back to my room, reinstated the offensive sentence and pressed 'send'.

A couple of days later, M. Audier emailed to say he would deal with my question in the next class. He also set out details of other examination requirements.

I was glad I asked.

I sat in the class as M. Audier provided a detailed explanation of what he required. While I didn't understand everything he said, I was aware that the exam consisted of analysing a paragraph from one of the textbooks we had studied.

The first element of the commentary was to identify the textbook from where the passage was drawn. This meant I had to read every text thoroughly. The place of the text in the book must be identified and its context. The ideas expressed were to be analysed and compared with competing or similar ideas. The commentary must end with a conclusion. The explanation by M. Audier was quite long and I doubt that I have accurately expressed what he said. At least I knew I had to thoroughly read every textbook he referred to in the semester.

I had been meeting Brenda regularly at Gare du Nord, however this Wednesday I changed the venue to Gare de L'est as I decided to surprise her, and take her to lunch to a restaurant near my apartment. Brenda arrived, in uniform, as agreed. I had my laptop slung over my shoulder. The restaurant near Damien's apartment was small, intimate and quite private. I suggested we have lunch. Brenda looked at the menu, seemed confused and ordered food that she barely touched. I felt uncomfortable and a bit guilty as I realised that Brenda was sitting and eating in a very foreign environment.

I opened my laptop and put it on the table and asked Brenda, "Would you like to see where you grew up?"

"Yes, but I have to go to Romania."

"No, I can show you on my computer. How do you spell where you grew up?"

I opened up Google Earth and searched for Arad. A picture of Arad filled the screen. I zoomed in and Brenda recognised places and streets. She pointed out the direction she wanted me to move the cursor. I moved it from street to street.

Brenda said, "C'est la!"

I zoomed into the abandoned building where Brenda grew up. She was engrossed in what she was seeing. I saw the look of joy on her lips, the sadness in her eyes and I sensed abandonment and loneliness.

She asked me to show her how to move the cursor. She spent some time exploring her town. She navigated her way around Arad, moving the cursor up, down, sideways, zoomed in and out. Differing emotions flitted across her face, her body tightened and relaxed; I wondered what she was remembering. She told me she wanted to buy her own house.

She got up and I gave her twenty euros. We parted company and as usual agreed to meet again at Gare du Nord.

The next week I sat for the Republique exam. I sat in my customary spot in the classroom. There was an empty chair as usual beside me. All my classmates sat in their own seats as we waited for M. Audier to issue the exam paper. I was relaxed and nervous. Relaxed because I was in M. Audier's class and nervous because the exam was about to start.

Anticipation caused me stress. My success would really depend on one thing and one thing alone. Would I recognise the text, who wrote it and the context in which it was written. The exam paper was placed face down in front of me, a writing booklet and scrap paper handed to me. M. Audier looked at me and gave me a faint smile.

M. Audier said, "Commencez."

I turned over the exam paper and read the short paragraph of text. This could be a small paragraph hidden in the literally hundreds of pages of text I had read. I read it and immediately recognised it. I knew Sir John Locke wrote it and where in the book it appeared. I could have almost identified the page number.

I picked up my pen then I put down my pen. I looked around the classroom. I observed every student in the room; no one was writing. I gazed at the ceiling and thought, *Where does this paragraph appear in the book, what is the theme, what is he saying about the theme, what did other philosophers say about this theme, what do I think?*

I used the scrap paper provided to plan. Ten minutes later I started to write.

I thought before I wrote a sentence. The sentences were short so there was every chance they were grammatically accurate. I wrote slowly and carefully. At the completion of the exam I handed in a single booklet.

The next day I had a Generale Culture exam. I really enjoyed this subject, although I would never have guessed its content before I started. The exam consisted of a large number of questions to which short answers were required. I carried my attitude in the Republique exam into the Generale Culture exam room. I looked at each question carefully, thought before I answered, and wrote simple French sentences. There was no philosophical analysis, just a regurgitation of knowledge. I was very confident in my knowledge and believed I passed.

I continued to regularly meet Brenda at Gare du Nord. I learnt that she earnt fifteen to twenty euros a day, asking for money from strangers. She was now living with her sister and her boyfriend and found it difficult. She said that she had an X-ray that showed she had breast cancer. She missed a week because she was having an operation. She said the operation was very expensive but she didn't ask me to pay for it. Our meetings became a ritual, if only for a short period. We would meet at the café, she would lead me into the shop next door and I would buy her cigarettes. She stopped bringing her daughter and we would chat with Brenda blowing smoke in my face. I gave up trying to persuade Brenda to show me how she foraged for food. We always parted with au revoir and the words "a la semaine".

After the exam in the Republique and Culture Generale I became quite settled. I had a routine of study; I spent an hour a week with Brenda, I gave up badminton and going to the gym in St. Germaine. I either studied in my room or went to the library at Port Clingancourt. I ate at Fahat's restaurant every day. One day I walked into the restaurant and he, unusually, was alone. Typically when I arrived for lunch there would be up to half a dozen old men seated around the restaurant. He would announce in a booming voice, "Here comes the oldest student at the Sorbonne." This was the signal for the huge Alsation dog sleeping behind the bar to awaken and amble towards me for its customary pat behind the ears. I had met Fahat's wife, daughter and son. I was always welcomed. We talked about Australia, his background and our families. Our conversation was difficult and stilted. He talked of animals. In Australia there was the kangaroo, in his country there are the chameaux.

"What is a chameau?"

"Fumer," he said.

I knew straight away. Fumer is to smoke and Camel cigarettes have a picture of a camel on the packet.

This particular day he was alone in the restaurant and he greeted me with bonjour. As I sat down and the dog put its head on my lap, Farid sat beside me.

"I am sorry I was angry when you first came," he said. His face reflected sadness and regret. His unnecessary apology was very moving. He didn't know how important his welcoming smile and friendship was in providing me with a safe haven during my days at university.

"That's OK. I understand your problems," was an inadequate response but was the best I could manage at the time.

The other constant in my life was the woman on the street. Every day I walked past her on the way to the library, every day we exchanged bonjours. I never gave her money. I was still angry about the last fiasco when I was harassed by her family. Sometimes I bent down and held the toddler's hand or stroked her head before continuing to the library. It never occurred to me that this was offensive or that a stranger patting a child's head was intrusive.

My anger soon subsided and I relented. I asked her what she wanted. We went into the supermarket to buy some nappies and wipes. While she chose the nappies a woman shopper said, "Vous êtes très gentile (you are very kind)." The Romanian woman was very grateful for the nappies and wipes. I refused to let her buy food from the shelves except for some chewing gum at the counter. As before, the woman at the checkout counter scowled at both of us as I paid for the products.

Twenty-five

October and November came and went and in mid-December the Philosophy Generale oral exam quickly came upon me. I wasn't particularly concerned, I was understanding more, reading the textbooks quickly and could read and understand most of *Le Parisien*.

When I entered the exam room there were five students sitting down. I had figured out that as one person completed the oral exam and left the room, another student replaced that student. I approached the examiner at the front of the room.

"Choissez deux chiffre entre une et trente," she said.

I thought she wanted me to choose two numbers between one and thirty, but I wasn't sure and didn't want to make a fool of myself. What could choosing two numbers have to do with this exam, I thought.

"Repetez s'il vous plait?" I said.

She repeated it.

"Je ne comprend pas," I replied.

She repeated again what she said, and I stood in front of her utterly confused.

There was an awkward silence. The examiner was not

going to communicate in English and I was not going respond to her request.

"She wants you to choose two numbers between one and thirty," a student called from the back of the class.

I chose two numbers and she gave me two pieces of paper each with a question on it and said I must answer one question.

"Comprenez vous?"

I told her I had to answer one question, and she said I had half an hour (which was now twenty-five minutes) to prepare the question.

I chose "Can we communicate our experience?" I knew what the philosophers said about this subject but I was blissfully unaware of the method I must use to answer the question. Ignorance is bliss, and I believed I had the requisite knowledge.

I was called to the front and sat before the examiner.

"Commencez," she said.

I confidently started to answer the question. I had barely been speaking for twenty seconds when I was interrupted by the examiner speaking, of course, in French.

"You must do this in French, not English."

"I am speaking French."

There was muffled laughter from the students in the room.

I quickly realised the problem. I recommenced. I spoke slowly, clearly and enunciated with some exaggeration each syllable. At the end of the presentation the examiner said she understood me.

The Philosophy Generale exam was a wake-up call; my opinion of my grasp of French far exceeded reality. I had two essays to hand in and two more exams in the next six days. I was functioning at a high level. This was not unusual—when I am not depressed I can work long hours under sustained pressure. I had gradually climbed out of the emotional and mental nadir I was in at the end of October, and now six weeks later, had recovered, to the extent that I am ever able. Yes, I had to deal with an extraordinary workload, but as Hume would say, we are our experience and I had been there before.

After I left the New South Wales Department of Education I studied law at the Australian National University. To support myself, I taught at Canberra Grammar School where I lived as a boarding house master. I resigned from Canberra Grammar after three years to concentrate on full-time law studies. By that stage I was halfway through the subjects I needed to pass third-year law.

Law at the ANU was a four-year course. I tried to enrol in all nine subjects I needed to complete third year and the final year of the degree. I wanted to finish the law degree in one year. The ANU refused to enrol me in all the subjects.

I made an appointment to see the dean. As a witness in court would say, to the best of my recollection, the following conversation took place:

"I want to do nine subjects to complete my law degree and my enrolment has been refused," I said.

"The rules are very explicit. You are not permitted to take nine subjects. The maximum allowable is six."

"What rule are you talking about?"

"The rule that renders a prohibition on undergraduates enrolling in excess of six subjects," the dean said.

"I am not an undergraduate, I am a graduate. I have an economics degree from Sydney University."

"You are required to be a graduate of the ANU."

"I suppose you can point me to the exact rule that defines a graduate as being a graduate of the ANU?"

"No, the inference is un-contestable," he said a little testily.

"So, what you're saying is that in every corner of the globe I am a graduate, but the moment I step inside the hallowed gates of the ANU I am not a graduate."

The conversation continued back and forth. I discussed the possibility of appealing to the university senate. The dean suddenly said, "I will exercise my discretion and permit you to enrol in nine subjects. You will be enrolled in some of the most difficult law subjects and you undoubtedly will fail." He rose from his chair signalling our meeting had ended.

I set myself a very strict timetable. I arrived at the university every day at nine a.m. and left the library at ten p.m. I made sure that I studied the reading for every lecture. Every holiday between semesters the routine remained the same. I gave myself an hour for lunch. Every lunchtime I ran for half an hour, had a shower and ate. Dinner was between six and seven o'clock.

I was elected as a student representative to the law faculty council. I represented the law school in the interfaculty moot competition in Perth. I enthusiastically participated in all lectures, completed all assignments and was always prepared to answer questions lecturers posed in class.

I suspected my run-in with the dean was common knowledge among university staff. Before one exam a lecturer asked to see me in his office. He asked my opinion on various legal problems. We discussed the problems at some length. I wondered why a lecturer would want the opinion of a student. When the same questions were on the exam paper I found our discussion very helpful.

I walked out of another exam and the distinguished professor who taught me asked how I went.

I said, "I am not sure."

"Did you write your name on the top of the paper?"

"Yes."

"In that case, Russell, you passed."

I did very well in all subjects, except Property II, which I was lucky to pass.

I had to make hard decisions as to how to allocate my time. I met Brenda, in uniform, the same boots and jacket, at Gare du Nord. As usual I bought her cigarettes and she blew smoke in my face as we chatted. The "vous comprenez?" and "je ne comprend pas" were now less frequent. I was used to Brenda's accent and my language skills had greatly improved.

I told Brenda about my upcoming university commitments and that I couldn't see her again. We walked to the corner. For the first time I didn't offer her money and she didn't ask for any.

"What are you going to do?" I asked.

"Ask people for money."

We exchanged au revoirs.

Pensively I walked towards Gare du Nord. Brenda and I always used the formal "vous". We never greeted each other with the customary kiss on the cheek, there was no physical contact, not even a handshake, and no real warmth. In a way, we used each other to satisfy our needs whether they be financial or emotional. I was not sure what my needs were, all I knew is that when we were together my heartrate fell and the tension in my shoulders disappeared.

I stopped, turned around, and saw her in the near distance. She was approaching a stranger. I saw her purple boots. I turned away, and never saw her again.

Twenty-six

It was an unusual day. I had just survived yet another M. Kammerer tutorial. I lived in constant fear of the questions he might ask. I understood the beginning and end of his lessons very well; *bonjour* and *a la semaine*. However, I was reading more quickly and in the context of what I had read, and M. Ludwig's lectures, I had some idea of what he was teaching.

I left the class and was walking towards the exit when a student came from behind and says *bonjour*. I recognised him from my class.

"Excuse me sir, do you know we have an exam next week?"

"An exam in what?"

"M. Kammerer said we have an exam next week."

Of course I had no idea we had an exam next week. The student explained the topics we'd be examined on. I was grateful for his intervention as I now had time to prepare, but it was an exam I had not counted on.

I prepared well for the exam. I was fortunate I had M. Ludwig as a lecturer. M. Ludwig was just as friendly and good humoured as when I met him for my enrolment. His method was chalk and cheese to M. Kammerer. I sat for the exam and knew that I passed easily. The questions were knowledge questions, not difficult and I knew the answers.

The next week M. Kammerer handed me my exam paper in class. I had scored twenty-five percent. I looked at my paper again. Yes, I had received twenty-five percent. I pondered this result. I received no notice of the previous exam and scored thirty-five percent. This exam I knew was coming, prepared well and scored twenty-five percent. I decided I must set realistic goals. If I worked really hard and fully understood the subject, next exam I should score ten percent.

M. Kammerer put model answers on the whiteboard. I believed that I answered the questions in accordance with his model answers. I noted that parts of my papers had not been marked. I was given nought out of ten for orthography.

After the tutorial later in the day I walked along the top level of the university. The corridor was quite narrow and there was considerable student traffic. I noticed M. Kammerer walking towards me. He approached directly in front of me. He stepped to the left and I stepped to the right. We were face to face and I was angry.

I looked him in the eye and glowered.

"You gave me zero for orthography—what is orthography?"

M. Kammerer proceeded to give me a detailed explanation in French of what orthography was. My French had improved to the extent I understood him. He said that orthography was the way I set out my answer. The answers must be neat, have no crossing out and proper paragraphs, excellent grammar and expression. I thought to myself, *if I knew that, I would have brought my colouring-in pencils.*

I knew that my answer was scrawled, my handwriting appalling and the paper looked like a dog's breakfast.

He then said, "Vous comprenez?"

"No."

"Okay. We will do this in English."

He then repeated in English what I already understood in French.

I was vaguely aware of students standing in the vicinity. M. Kammerer and I were standing quite close to each other. The flow of students around us slowed down.

I said, "Giving me zero for orthography is not fair. I am an international student. How can I compete with a French student?"

"That's the way it is."

I was agitated. "Why should a French student automatically be given more marks than me? It is hard enough as it is, without being penalised because I don't happen to be French!"

I was aware the crowd had grown. I knew very few French students admitted to speaking English. I presumed the students listening wanted to improve their English language skills.

"I know it is unfair, but that's the way it is."

I was now very annoyed.

"I notice you didn't even mark some of my exam," I said.

"No, I didn't. Your writing is illegible."

"OK, I will write it out again clearly, so you can mark it."

"No, you can't do that."

"Why not? I thought I came to the Sorbonne to be marked on what I know, I didn't know it was a handwriting test."

"It wouldn't be fair to other students."

"That's not right. You marked every other student's exam and marked them on what they knew. All I am asking is that I rewrite my exam paper, word for word, comma for comma, error for error. What's unfair about that?!"

"All right then, you can rewrite it but I will not promise I will change your mark."

He continued, pointing his finger at my chest: "You have a big problem, monsieur. If you want to pass exams at the Sorbonne, you need to think more and write less. Keep your sentences short, think before you write. You're here to think, not write volumes of useless information. I also suggest you learn to write legibly and clearly."

"Thanks, M. Kammerer," I said with a voice laden with sarcasm.

He stepped to one side and continued on his way.

Later that day I was standing on the Metro platform at Port Clingancourt. Two students approached me. One student asked if I was Australian. When I said yes, he recounted his happy experience at Adelaide University. Both students had tutorials with M. Kammerer, but they were not in my tutor group.

They asked me about my problems with M. Kammerer and I explained my predicament. They were both very uncomplimentary about M. Kammerer. I thought this was a shame. I believed the apparent dislike of M. Kammerer was due to his holding students accountable. He really cared. He continually urged students to study, and suggested they form groups to discuss the course.

I had won the battle but may well have lost the war. I could also count. On the heroic assumption that M. Kammerer would increase my mark, the difference it would make to my chances of passing the subject was miniscule. My time was much better spent studying the textbooks than rewriting the exam. I beat a hasty and ignominious retreat.

I sent an email to M. Kammerer. I apologised for being *bouleverser* (upset). I would not rewrite the exam. I was at the Sorbonne to learn and marks were not important. I added that when I took exams I would think before I wrote and would write clearly and precisely.

M. Kammerer replied immediately. He was happy I changed my ways and that was his goal. He wished me every success and suggested I write to him if I had any other problem. I responded very positively to M. Kammerer's tough love. He might not be the teacher I wanted, but he was the teacher I needed.

In between M. Kammerer's exam and my confrontation I had become unsettled. I was no longer seeing Brenda, not venturing into the city and spending more time in the library. Every day I saw Fahat and passed the woman on the street. One day she was no longer there. I walked past where she sat and noticed the empty space. My path from the station to the library was concrete and bitumen, all of it the same, nothing to distinguish one piece of concrete from the other. Yet when I passed this particular piece of concrete it was not like any other piece of concrete. It meant something, and whatever it meant, I missed it. As I walked past I had images of the dilapidated old pram, with the baby sometimes snug inside, sometimes being breastfed, and the baby sometimes playing on the footpath. I missed stroking the baby's head and saying "bonjour".

Twenty-seven

I walked into the room for the final art exam and sat down. Anne was in front of me and she turned and gave me the thumbs up. Marion, her friend, who was part of a group I regularly chatted to on the platform of Port de Clingancourt, turned and smiled. I smiled back. I was extremely confident as Mme Blanc-Benon issued the exam papers.

I had studied very hard. A month prior, Marion sent me a bibliography of all the readings for the subject and the relevant chapters. I read and absorbed all the material. The one exception was Hegel, a notoriously difficult philosopher, but Nicolai explained the difficult parts of the text during our weekly tutorial sessions. Nicolai had no knowledge of Hegel as a philosopher but he could read and understand a particular text.

I was really well prepared except that I had not had the benefit of M. Kammerer's finger-pointing reality check—this occurred a couple of days later. Mme Blanc-Benon issued the exam questions and a booklet to write the answers. She also distributed small sheets of scrap paper I didn't use. We were given ten minutes reading time. I looked at the questions and considered the choices as to which questions to answer—it didn't matter; I could answer all questions, so I avoided Hegel.

Mme Blanc-Benon said, "Commencez."

I was like a hungry lion pouncing on the carcass of a tender antelope. I devoured the exam paper. I ripped and tore it to shreds. I wrote furiously, intent on making sure every inch of my knowledge appeared on the paper. I filled the booklet. I asked Mme Blanc-Benon for another booklet. She raised her eyebrows when I asked for a third booklet. I wrote furiously and just finished when the exam time ended.

Mme Blanc-Benon collected the booklets from each student. I was euphoric. I knew I had done brilliantly.

I sent an email to Anne, very cautious, written in English.

I hope this email does not embarrass you—it certainly is not intended to. I owe you big time. I have my last exam before Xmas on the 19th December. I fly back to Australia the next day. I have bought 2 tickets to see Sister Act on the 19th December at 8 p.m. I bought 2 tickets because I do not want to go by myself. Would you be interested in seeing this show? I know that when you helped me you expected nothing in return, however, if this show is something you would like to see and you are not doing anything else the seat is there for you.

She loved the show. I of course bought her a drink and ice cream during interval. While enthusiasm was not the sole preserve of the young, my life was happy being in the presence of the enthusiastic young woman who had helped me so much. As we stood outside the theatre at the end of the show, she said, "I would like to have coffee with you and have a long chat but I can't. I have been working really hard and my boyfriend is pissed that he hasn't seen me. He didn't want me to come here tonight. I'm sorry."

"That's fine, Anne. Thanks for coming with me, I really enjoyed it."

It didn't cross my mind that Anne would want to spend time with me. I wanted to show her I appreciated what she had done for me. Then again, why wouldn't she enjoy being with me, and having a nice chat about nothing in particular? My daughters liked my company.

At the end of the semester I decided to skip M. Rogove's last tutorial. I was studying at the university and went to the room at the end of his tutorial to apologise for my absence and to thank him for his help during the year.

I caught up with him in the corridor. He told me I had just missed a compulsory final exam and had not handed in an essay, also compulsory. As M. Rogove stood in front of me I was concerned he would behave like M. Kammerer. I felt failure was certain.

"When were we told about the exam?" I said.

"Two weeks ago, in class."

"I didn't hear you say that."

"Didn't you get an email?"

"No."

"It's on the student noticeboard."

"No, it's not."

M. Rogove asked me to come upstairs so he could show me the notification on the student noticeboard. I knew what he would find, or rather, what he wouldn't find.

M. Rogove searched in vain for the notice of the exam. As he searched, a secretary approached him and asked him if he needed help. He asked her whether or not students were notified by email of exams. She told him that students were not given notification of any exams or essays emanating from tutorials.

M. Rogove's response was immediate. He told me I could sit the exam the next day in another class he was conducting and I could hand the essay in after I returned to university after the Christmas break. It was exactly what I expected from M. Rogove.

I turned up the next day for the exam. I was grateful for this opportunity to sit the exam, even though he was giving a normal lecture. I was able to totally block out the distraction and I had the benefit of M. Kammerer's ruthless guidance as to how to answer examination questions at the Sorbonne.

Thanks to M. Kammerer, I carefully read the question. I then planned the answer. It was typical Sorbonne; I stated the problem, discussed the paradoxes, illustrated the paradoxes by reference to various philosophers and then drew my own conclusion. My writing, which was now a form of printing, was clear and legible. Would I pass? I didn't have a clue.

It was my final exam for the year and I proceeded to walk from the university to the library. Ten days earlier the woman on the street had suddenly reappeared. I felt better each day as I walked past and occasionally I dropped a euro in her cup. As I approached her I realised it would be the last time I would see her so, in a fit of generosity, I gave her ten euros, a large sum of money. She looked at me blandly, unsmiling, a face tinged with sadness. "Pour manger (to eat)" and then "nettoyage (to clean)," she softly and hesitantly said.

I was taken aback by her response, but contrary to my natural instincts, I said, "oui." She followed me into the supermarket. As usual she left the toddler in the pram at the entrance and grabbed a shopping basket.

When we reached the nappy section she tentatively put her hand towards the largest packet of nappies. I nodded my head. She grabbed the nappies and I put another packet the same size in the basket. She then wanted wipes and once again I bought more than she asked for. She chose food and miscellaneous personal items. On occasions she hesitantly moved her hand towards an object, and pulled it from the shelf when I nodded my head.

When we reached the footpath outside the shop, she turned and moved towards me. Our faces were inches apart. She was beaming. She had a huge smile on her face and was saying something I didn't understand. She was very close so I could only see her face. She had a flawless unlined forehead, dancing eyes and a lovely smile. She was beautiful.

Twenty-eight

I enjoyed living in Paris in December. The middle of winter was different to anything else I had experienced. The footpath outside Damien's apartment was covered in ice; I slipped, skated and survived travelling to the Gare de L'Est each morning. It was cold but dry with little wind, not unpleasant, as the skies were blue, the sun weak and warm. I always intended to be home for Christmas, the first in our new home. I was looking forward to going home and seeing Josie, my children and grandchildren.

I had my own key to Damien's apartment and my access at any time was unrestricted. On the 23rd December, I put my key in the lock, turned it and tried to open the door. A chain attached to the inside of the door prevented me from entering. I knocked, and knocked again. I heard the lounge room door open and shut. The chain was removed and the door opened to reveal Damien in a rather fetching pair of shorty pyjamas. Damien apologised profusely and said it was an accident.

I was quite insouciant, but my subconscious noted Damien head into the lounge and shut the door, thus prohibiting my entry, rather than going to bed. Perhaps he was watching a late-night movie.

An hour later I got up and went to the kitchen to quench my thirst. The kitchen and the lounge room had a common wall that was very thin. I heard sounds coming from the lounge room. At first, I thought it was the television, however, as cold water retreated down my throat I detected the sound of two male voices. The voices were muffled but were clearly male. At three a.m. I was awakened by the sound of running water. Someone was having a shower. Ten minutes later the front door was shut with a soft clang.

I greeted Damien in the morning. The lounge room door was open and I didn't detect anyone else in the apartment. My mind travelled back to a same-sex male couple who had influenced my attitude to homosexuality.

In the mid nineteen-seventies, I was practising as a conveyancing lawyer. Unusually, two men made an appointment to see me with respect to buying a property. I had never before acted for two men in this way.

Les and Gordon sat down. Les was the bigger of the two and not much older than me. He was of medium build and medium height, his distinguishing features being his large ears and prominent nose. Gordon was smaller, about the same age and appeared reserved and a bit shy. I chatted with them and they told me about the delicatessen they owned in Kogarah. Les did most of the talking, but after a while Gordon relaxed and contributed more to the conversation. They told me about the food they sold, the types of people they met and how they enjoyed what they were doing.

I really liked Les and Gordon. They were friendly, open and engaged with me. Above all I liked them as a couple. They were buying a home unit in Oatley, and I went through all aspects of the contract. I discussed where the finance was coming from and when they wanted to settle. I was not conscious of this at the time, but they were like a typical married couple. I would ask a question and Les usually answered. After answering, he asked Gordon if he agreed and respectfully listened to Gordon's opinion.

One of the key issues when two people bought property together was how the title was to be held. There were two options; joint tenancy and tenants in common. With joint tenancy both parties were listed as owners on the certificate of title and when one party died the other party became sole owner of the property. Even if the will of the deceased party gave all that party's assets to someone else, the property still went to the survivor. With tenants in common both parties were noted on the title, and each party had a separate, not necessarily equal, share of the property. When one party died, that party's share of the property went to the deceased party's next of kin or in accordance with the deceased's last will and testament.

Husbands and wives typically owned property as joint tenants, friends typically as tenants in common. My practice with husbands and wives was to first explain joint tenancy, as this is what I expected to happen. With friends, I first explained tenants in common. I asked Les and Gordon if they intended to buy the property as joint tenants, as I thought that's what they wanted.

My regard and respect for Les and Gordon was a backdrop to another experience that left me devastated. I was a member of the St. George Sutherland Law Society and was part of a trip organised to Hawaii. The trip included Oahu, The Big Island and Maui. Essential to the trip, in order to obtain a tax deduction for the cost, was attendance at lectures, presented by other lawyers. These lectures could just as easily have been presented in the Hurstville Civic Centre.

For the first part of the trip we stayed in the Rainbow Tower of the Hawaiian Hilton Hotel. It was a magnificent hotel, standing on the edge of Waikiki Beach. The first lecture, delivered by Justice David Yeldham, was held in a conference room overlooking Waikiki Beach.

In the early 1970s judges were considered remote and aloof. Solicitors such as myself had no opportunity to meet judges and my only contact with the judiciary occurred when I conducted court cases over which they presided. These individuals were often prickly and intolerant of what they saw as professional incompetence. I didn't like them much and it suited me not to have anything to do with them. Even so, I respected them as they represented the pinnacle of the legal profession. I travelled to Hawaii with my solicitor colleagues with a determination to learn. As with any form of learning sometimes there is conflict.

Unfortunately, Justice Yeldham's lecture coincided with another lesson I needed to attend. While Justice Yeldham was lecturing on the indefeasibility of Torrens title I was lying on a surfboard on Waikiki Beach. The instructor stood beside me as he showed me how to paddle on dry land. Stage two of the lesson comprised, from a prone position, of placing my hands beside my stomach and jumping to my feet to maintain a sideways standing position on the surfboard. Within an hour I became very adept at jumping to my feet and standing on a stationary surfboard on the sand.

Two hours later we were all at lunch. I was seated next to His Honour. It was the first time that I had talked socially with a judge. Justice Yeldham was great company over lunch—he was interested in where I lived, where I practised, and what

I wanted to do and see. I was mortified when he told me that his lecture had been interrupted by everyone rushing to the window to watch me stand on a stationary surfboard. Suddenly he tapped the table to get everyone's attention. Of course, when a judge taps, silence and attention are immediate.

"As you all know, a couple of hours ago, we had the opportunity to watch Russell demonstrate his formidable surfing skills. I thought on behalf of all his colleagues we might say to Russell that his surfing ability far exceeds his skills and knowledge as a lawyer."

The rest of His Honour's observations about my relative legal and surfing skills were drowned by laughter. I took it as a good-natured admonition for missing his lecture.

A few nights later, we were in a bar with His Honour. As the beer flowed and camaraderie evolved, three national groups—British, Australian and American—raucously sang their national anthems—except we sang *Waltzing Matilda*.

There was much we didn't know about David Yeldham. When he was appointed a judge not long before our trip away, David Yeldham was paying men for sex. Until 1984 homosexual acts were illegal in Australia, punishable by fourteen years jail. The risks that the judge took were enormous. Police trapped homosexuals. They would offer inducements for homosexual acts and arrest persons who responded. David Yeldham was caught on a few occasions and never charged.

In 1996 Franca Arena, the mother of two gay sons, under parliamentary privilege, insinuated that the judge, by then retired, was a paedophile. It was totally false; an outrageous abuse of parliamentary privilege. In November 1996, David Yeldham, a loving husband, father and grandfather, killed himself.

I was devastated by his death. I remembered the man I admired on our trip to Hawaii twenty years before. His sexual proclivities were of no interest to me; I only remembered the approachable, good-natured judge.

I lay in bed thinking of Les and Gordon, David Yeldham and Damien. I hoped Damien was with Pierre. I liked Pierre. Whenever I saw Pierre he always smiled, was happy to see me, spoke to me in French, and wanted to know what I was studying. Damien was a much nicer and happier person when he was with Pierre.

Twenty-nine

My flight home from the Paris winter was uneventful. A limousine to the airport, no check-in queues, and priority security and customs clearance made an easy start to the journey. I flew Emirates and enjoyed the lounge in Dubai. A huge space with first-class restaurant-type food and brilliant service but above all a huge shallow pool which emitted the sound of running water exuding an air of peace and tranquility. Josie picked me up from the airport as she always did. Whenever I travelled overseas Josie insisted she both take me and pick me up. I was never at the mercy of taxis.

I settled quickly back home into the Australian summer. Our home was somewhat of an open house. Josie's parents had six children born and raised in Australia. When I first met Josie's parents, Hoop and Yep, I was struck by their hospitality. Josie never knocked on the door. The door was never locked and family came and went as if they lived there. Josie was the same. Our house was open; she was never too tired nor too occupied to welcome family. Four children and nine grandchildren inhabited our home, particularly in summer. I had built a self-contained flat underneath the house and our daughter Mel, her husband Dylan and two children lived there. I believed in the concept of the extended family, working on the basis that family was close but independent. I was fortunate that the waterfront, large pool and boating facilities attracted frequent visits from my kids and my grandkids.

I was a world away from Paris. I loved being home but couldn't wait to go back. Sitting on the waterfront, seeing my friends, doing things with my family relaxed and rejuvenated me. As I relaxed, the pressures and problems of study became such a distant memory that within a week I became restless, and looked forward to returning to Paris to finish my exams.

My first exam was Philosophie Moderne. It was the most difficult subject compounded by the fact that I had not had much help from Nicolai. As my understanding improved I now enjoyed Descartes, however the subject was intellectually very difficult. The problem was that I was not aware of my problems in understanding the concepts.

The exam was in a lecture theatre filled with well over one hundred students. All students were instructed to leave bags and telephones at the front desk. In a rare concession to international students I was allowed to take a dictionary into the exam. I used an app on my mobile phone as a dictionary. I asked one of the staff if I could have access to a paper dictionary but I was told there wasn't a dictionary available. I asked if I could take my mobile phone into the exam but the request was refused. I asked to speak to a supervisor.

"Bonjour Monsieur, I am an international student and I know I am allowed to take a dictionary into the exam. I don't have a paper dictionary so I need to use the dictionary on my mobile phone. Can I keep my mobile phone?"

"No, mobile phones are not allowed in the exam room."

As the supervisor was speaking Marion stood beside me. She didn't say anything.

I replied, "What is your name please, sir?"

"Why do you want to know?"

"Because I want to write in large letters on the front of the exam paper your name and your refusal to let me use the dictionary on my phone."

He relented so I kept my phone.

Another person took my handbag and explained where she was storing it. I told her that I understood. Marion moved to her seat.

This final written exam was based on an obscure passage from Descartes' sixth meditation and was very difficult. I had read the passage, I knew where it was in the sixth meditation and I understood it. I shared my knowledge, without analysis, with the examiner. I later exchanged emails with Anne who described the extract as "very tricky". I was pleased that at least I wrote clearly.

It was January and very cold in Paris. I sat alone in a restaurant I had never before frequented. It was strange that I was starting to feel disconnected from my previous habits and routines. Perhaps subconsciously, by eating in a strange restaurant, I was emotionally preparing myself to leave Paris and the Sorbonne forever. I reflected on my exam and felt downhearted that I had failed to absorb the lessons M. Kammerer and M. Slama had given me. I felt that I had let both of my teachers down. They went out of their way to help me and I failed to absorb simple and obvious lessons.

I brightened up. I had more exams and I would not repeat my mistakes. My best subject was yet to come.

I was relaxed before the History of the Philosophy of Science exam. M. Ludwig was his usual jovial self; happy, friendly and good-humoured. It could have been the start of a picnic rather than an exam, although there was somewhat an air of seriousness.

The exam papers were issued and I found the exam very easy. The subject didn't have the conceptual difficulties of other subjects and as its name suggests was history. At the higher level of understanding of course it was conceptually difficult, however there was little difficulty in the basic concepts. I thought before I wrote, and wrote short legible sentences. The only thing standing between my success and failure was my level of written French.

My final task was to hand in an essay on Nietzsche. The essay was on the connection between truth and experience. Nietzsche coined the phrase "That which does not kill us, makes us stronger." What struck me was the relevance of Nietzsche to my own circumstances. I didn't know it at the time but years earlier I had followed Nietzsche's philosophy. Studying at the Sorbonne showed me the philosophical basis on which my attitude to life had been transformed.

In 1992 after I was evicted from my home I lived in rented premises. I established a legal practice in my bedroom and set about surviving. My friends Bob and Vicki suggested I do a Forum course.

When Vicki suggested something would be beneficial for me I took notice. It was a weekend residential course. There was no doubt that the course provided great benefits to participants who approached the course with an open mind. Of course, whether or not an open mind made a person susceptible to indoctrination was another question.

Forum asserted that everything existed in language. All our knowledge was represented in words. We looked at a rock, what was it? If it didn't have a word then it didn't exist. This particularly applied to values. Values were created in language.

The idea that same-sex couples should be allowed to marry was a relatively modern concept now expressed in language as "marriage for all".

"Everything known to man was contained in the language, in other words nothing existed outside of language. Through language man has created a building that contains a set of rules of behavior." (Nietzsche)

The Forum lecturer drew a box on the whiteboard. He stated that each box had a label. Once we put a label on the box in which we lived we were restricted to living within that box. It was the box and the label that shut down our possibilities.

The analysis had a huge impact. The box I was incarcerated in was 'a solicitor'. During the course of the weekend I no longer saw myself as a solicitor. I saw myself as a person with a considerable degree of ability and skills. I believed that the loss of my wealth was an opportunity, not a problem. Instead of spending the next twenty or thirty years in a suburban solicitor's office I had a new and fresh start. I made a list of my debts and set about dealing with financial issues. Over the next couple of years, I solved the financial issues and within a short time thereafter was no longer a solicitor. Financial misfortune and Forum and Nietzsche created the catalyst for future experiences I would never otherwise have contemplated.

My exams finished and I had time to kill before I flew home. I had been in Paris six months and had not really explored it to any degree. I had ridden down the cobbled street leading to the Champs-Elysees on my bike and visited most of the major attractions, but not much else. I decided to visit the Basilica Sacre Coeur at Montmarte.

I walked to Gare de L'Est and took travel line 4 to Barbes Rochouart, and then line 2 to Anvers. The recommendation I had received was unusual. I knew an Australian who owned property in the South of France, constantly travelled to France and had a wide knowledge of French tourist places. We had had dinner together in November. He recommended a visit to the Sacre Coeur. Surprisingly, the Palace of Versailles, the Eiffel Tower and the Louvre were not part of his visit list. I trusted his judgement.

On reaching the street from the Metro Anvers the changes in population and streetscape were apparent. Dark-coloured people had retreated to the suburbs surrounding Saint-Denis and persons of Asian appearance congregated in the streets.

The street surrounding the exit to the station didn't have the ubiquitous Paris restaurant or brasserie. There was a fruit stall surrounded by a myriad of stores selling tourist gifts and trinkets. The sign to Sacre Coeur pointed up the hill. I walked up a pedestrian street, very narrow and crowded with tourists. Other than one or two eating places, four hundred metres of narrow road directed pedestrians between rows of establishments designed to separate tourists from their money.

The shops sold tablecloths, teatowels, posters and T-shirts. They sold anything that was possible on which to print a picture of the Basilica. There were of course other related tourist gifts, including models of the Eiffel Tower.

I walked up the hill to the street that ran along the bottom of the grounds on which the Basilica stood. The Basilica stood on the top of the hill. It was an imposing structure that dominated the skyline. A long winding footpath and steps cutting through large swathes of mown lawn took my eye ever upwards to the Basilica. Crowds of people wended their way slowly and ever wearily up the hill. I was fit and had nothing else to do; I wouldn't have a problem negotiating the route to the top of the hill.

I saw a line of men and woman patiently waiting. I stood in line for ten minutes, however as the line edged slowly forward, I realised it was the line to use the toilet not to buy a ticket to the funicular. I went to the funicular turnstile, realised my Navigo pass was valid, walked into the car and was carried to the top. Forty-two stairs later, fresh as a daisy, I stood at the foot of the Basilica. I turned my back and looked at Paris. Standing with my back to the Basilica gave me a sense of how extensive Paris was. The buildings of Paris stretched as far as the eye could see. My biggest impression was that the beautiful low-rise buildings appeared like a stony desert as a distant landscape. Small pockets of high-rise buildings rose in the distance.

I lined up to walk inside the Basilica of the Sacre Coeur. It was an impressive structure with high domed ceilings and alcoves with stained glass windows. I stood amongst the human throng, forbidden to take photos, speaking in strained whispers, craning necks to better view objects. The largely empty pews occupied most of the inside of the building.

I felt nothing. Was this a sanctuary, was it a place of worship, was it a sacred place? The external appearance, the signs on the wall, the religious paraphernalia answered yes. Yet there wasn't an uplifting of the soul, no feeling of the presence of God. The crowds of slowly moving people were present only to gawk, not worship; whatever this place represented, it was nothing more than an empty edifice.

I didn't last long inside the Basilica. I headed for the exit, past the demand for donations and into the open air. I walked around the building and veered left towards a restaurant. In one hundred metres, five artists wanted to paint my portrait. I understood why, with my distinctive features, I was an interesting subject but I didn't understand why I should pay to spend my time sitting with them.

I saw a rectangular square. On the edges, artists sat side by side displaying their artwork. Each artist offered to paint portraits for tourists. I walked between rows of artists. In the middle of the rectangle were market stalls selling all types of food and merchandise. It was different and interesting.

I settled to eat at Chez Plumeau, an attractive small restaurant set among trees and gardens. An old man sat nearby playing *Bridge over Troubled Water* on the violin. I ordered brochette de boeuf, salade and gaspacho de fruit rouges for dessert. This was washed down with a house red.

I sat relaxed, calm and happy, the familiar sounds of the violin penetrating my subconscious. I was happy, but with emptiness. What was I missing? The frenetic activity of my studies? My university teachers who were so kind to me? The students who helped me and engaged with me? The people I met on the street? Those I lived with? No.

I missed Josie.

I knew what we would be doing if Josie were here. Josie loves shopping but paradoxically does not like spending. Josie could shops for hours but only buys things we need. Our children and grandchildren say Josie buys the best presents. She loves looking.

We would be strolling through the market spending time at every stall. We would discuss whether or not my portrait should be painted. She wouldn't have any interest in her own portrait being painted. After my attention span waned, I would retreat to a bistro for a coffee and read the paper. She would return so I could mind some presents she had bought. After an hour or so she would say it was time for lunch. We would sit at the table where I was sitting now and talk about her purchases. Discuss what present she bought for which grandchild. We would talk about our day and our plans.

I sat at Chez Plumeau, happy and relaxed, but I couldn't wait to get home. I had finished my studies, the bee in my bonnet had flown away and there was nothing left for me in Paris.

I had one final chore and that was to bid adieu to Damien. The night before I left I took him to a restaurant of his choice. We dined at Les Enfants Perdus, a restaurant within walking distance of Damien's apartment.

The menu was eclectic and very expensive. Damien chose an entrée Le Foie gras De Canard: maison, maître au Porto et au cognac, chutney d'oignons et mangue. The French force-feed a duck so it becomes hugely fat, kill it and remove its liver. The liver was served as foie gras. The technique of force-feeding the duck was called gavage. The French government declared foie gras part of France's gastronomical heritage. I knew how the duck felt—I was being force-fed. Damien, while eating, had a rhythm. He cut into the food, placed it on his fork and into his mouth and commenced to chew. At the point where he was starting to digest the food he force-fed me stories. The entrée was his unreasonable estranged wife. I was better at digesting Hegel, Kant and Popper than Damien's stories.

Damien's main course was Le Boef: au filet 250gm pomme de terre sautés et purillees os anoisette, sauce au pauve. An excellent choice and the most expensive course on the menu. Romain, he said, was a lazy boy who refused to study and would never amount to anything.

Creme Brulee: decline, vanilla, praline and pistache. A beautiful creamy dessert washed down with a dose of Damien's stories about his sister's greed.

L'Ardoise de Fromage, a very extensive cheese plate, and a bottle of Poully Fuisse complemented perfectly a serving of how difficult French university was and how I would fail.

I was not sure who was the most difficult, Damien or me. Damien regularly had students stay with him. I wondered if I was no more than a necessary evil so that he could earn extra money to enhance his lifestyle.

On the one hand, he had been really helpful. Organising my rail pass, coming with me to outings with Romain and particularly my evening with Maraise. I felt underneath there was continuing tension. I resented his always speaking in English. This was a huge barrier in my relating to him. I subconsciously regarded it as rejection. I needed French language skills and he adamantly refused to help.

I didn't really like him, and he would never be my friend. Yelling at Romain, and his violence to others rendered me cautious in his presence. I could never really relax. I had to be careful what I said, although on occasions I crossed the line.

Without Damien's apartment and the safe, comfortable conditions, life would have been much more difficult in Paris. But I couldn't wait to leave Damien and I couldn't wait to see Josie.

Thirty

I arrived in Australia at the end of January. The hot summer sun was a dramatic change and a relief from the Paris winter. Josie picked me up from the airport as usual. I was happy to see her and glad to be home.

I arrived home happy that everything was normal. Josie had no difficulty in managing the household, paying the bills and looking after grandchildren. I guess that's because it's what she did anyway. I had a fairytale existence. I lived in a new waterfront home on Gunnamatta Bay, a happily married daughter with two young children lived independently downstairs, and I had a loving wife. I was fortunate to have acquired sufficient wealth that I didn't work for a living, and my investments were competently managed with the help of great managers and business partners. I resumed my gym program and settled into a day in which my major worry was how to complete the *Sydney Morning Herald*'s quick crossword, sudoku, Kenken and This Way and That. I resumed breakfast at Mim's each morning, I had few demands on my time; dealing with the town planner for my new jetty, a dispute with an electrical contractor, and the odd query regarding other investments were hardly time-consuming or challenging.

It was early February when I tried to obtain my exam results. I tried the students' internal web called the ENT. I was not able to access the ENT because I was no longer enrolled as a student. The university administration advised that I could inspect my exam papers at the end of January in Paris. Even if I wanted to go back it was too late.

I gradually learnt the differences between the Sorbonne and Sydney University. I attended the Sorbonne under the European Transfer Credit System (ETCS). This system enabled the Sorbonne to advise Sydney University how many credits I earned while studying at the Sorbonne. A full-time Sydney University student, passing every subject, obtained twenty-eight credit points. If a student failed a subject, less credit points were obtained and it took longer to graduate.

The Sorbonne did not require a student to pass all subjects. If a student had an average of fifty percent or more over all subjects, then the student progressed into the next semester. No subject had to be repeated, and there was no penalty for failing a subject. I studied five subjects at the Sorbonne plus two options, Badminton and Advanced Writing, that I hoped translated to twenty-eight credit points at Sydney University. Strangely, I had to study six subjects at Sydney University to earn twenty-eight credits points.

The Sorbonne scored every subject out of twenty, so five subjects amounted to one hundred; I needed to score fifty to pass. I was aghast when I received my results.

RESULTS

Subject	Mark Breakup	Final Mark
Philosophie Generale		10/20
Oral exam	7/20	
Final exam	13/20	
Total	10/20	
Philosophie de l'Art		8.5/20
Total	8.5/20	
Philosophie des Sciences		13.5/20
Mr. Kammerer tut.	8.5/20	
Final science exam	16/20	
Culture final exam	16/20	
Total	13.5/20	
Philosophie Moderne		7.5/20
Slama exam	7/20	
Final exam	8/20	
Total	7.5/20	
Cours d'ouverture		14.5/20
Total	14.5/20	
Grand Total		**54/100**

I was very upset by these results so I asked M. Ludwig if they could be reviewed. He agreed to a review and congratulated me on my marks in his subjects. M. Ludwig suggested I contact Mme Blanc-Benon directly regarding my Art exam in which I scored a total of 8.5/20. I sent her the following email:

Hello Mme,

I appreciated your classes, and I appreciate all the help you have given me. I was very disappointed with my final grade. I thought I had a lot of knowledge. In the philosophy and history of science final exams my grade was 16/20 and general culture 16/20 and 14.5/20 in What is a Republic. I know you are very fair, and I would like to know where I went wrong. I was on the exchange for a single semester and I'm back in Sydney. I wish you all the best for the future. I will always remember your class.

Failure is not something I'm used to so I would like to know where I went wrong.

Regards.

Mme Blanc Benon replied,

I received your two messages but did not reply immediately because I had to get your copy by the secretary of Clignancourt where I do not teach this semester anymore. I was able to scan it. Your score is due to your language mistakes. I know that you have knowledge but when your text is simply incomprehensible I am, for my part, incapable of judging the content. I understand your disappointment but be aware that my mark did not imply any unfavorable judgement on your efforts and your involvement which were excellent.

Philosophy of Science and Culture General (Philosophie des sciences) counted as one subject. M. Kammerer's tutorials and the marks in the two final exams carried equal weight. M. Kammerer's mark was lead in the saddlebags.

Modern Philosophy was a problem. I accepted this as probably accurate although I challenged it. In a couple of long email exchanges with Mme Laurent she informed me that the mark reflected the standard and quality of my work. She pointed out my mark was of no consequence, as I passed the semester anyway.

My mark of 14.5/20 in the Republic (Cours d'ouverture) was no surprise.

In the context of my mental state at the time, these results reinforced all my insecurities and low self-esteem. When I enrolled at the Sorbonne, I expected, worst case, to pass every subject. I believed the results were poor, and that I was a failure. This wasn't true. I started the semester with poor language skills and no educational background in philosophy. Ongoing tests throughout the semester dragged down my final exam marks. My final exam marks where I competed on an even footing with French students in anonymously marked papers were excellent overall. I failed Art (47.5%) due to shocking exam technique not lack of knowledge. Ironically, I failed Philosophie Moderne (40%). I enjoyed Descartes and thought I had a clear knowledge of his philosophy. Descartes is famous for "I think therefore I am". In my case thinking is not what I was, my emotions were what I was. I never considered debating Descartes' philosophical premise with myself while I was studying. Perhaps I should have. I should have been proud, not devastated by my results.

I recovered from the depths of depression and despair in Paris to finish my studies relatively happy and settled. The results reflected failure and I spiralled downwards. I had no hobbies, no direction and time on my hands. I wasn't aware of self-reflection, I never lived in the present; my life was spent setting and achieving goals.

As February became March then April, the distance between life in Paris and my existence at home increased. In Paris, the point and purpose of trying to pass exams, the struggle to communicate and the everyday challenges kept me functioning. In Australia, my life was like a lid being removed from a pressure cooker. Suddenly there were no goals, nothing to achieve, no one needed me for anything. Depression was like canoeing in a river towards a waterfall. The river flowed rapidly, the canoeist was oblivious to the waterfall. Paddling was easy, the river picked up speed. Paddling was even easier, until the waterfall was reached and it was too late to bail out. I was oblivious to the impending waterfall, so much so that Josie and I booked a trip to Europe for the middle of the year, and I organised to spend time at Berrara with friends. I knew I had a problem, so I consulted the local doctor who diagnosed my depression, and gave me medication. My slide into depression during March was obvious; my children told me they were sad and worried to see me so down.

In April, I wrote a note to Josie and put it on the front seat of the Porsche alongside my mobile phone.

Hi Darling

I do not want anything. I am not going to access our bank account or change anything. I have cancelled Chris Penfold and Jarrod saving $100 per week. No more Mim's another $150 per week saved.

I have no home—to go somewhere else will only change the residence of my unhappiness.

I will live on the street—I hope I can achieve something for others. I have no identification or credit cards and have adopted a new name.

I will be OK.

Love

Russell xx

P.S. There is no one else, today's relationship is tomorrow's heartache.

I had no plans, no concept of what I was going to do nor where I was going, except to the city. I couldn't explain why I did it, any more than a dog would know why it pissed against a particular telegraph pole.

Descartes postulated that animals lacked reason although they acted in accordance with the general rules of reason.

When a kingfisher dived into a pond to catch a fish it instinctively adjusted for light refraction, even though it had never heard of Snell's law. Animals, however, couldn't act on general principles that could be used in all kinds of situations, and at this time neither could I. When I fled from home my reasoning capability was little better than that of a dog, so that I could only act within the general rules of reason. It was instinct.

I emptied my pockets, except for four hundred dollars in cash and Aropax anti-depressant tablets, which I removed from the box that had my name on it. I got off at Martin Place station and wandered aimlessly towards the Domain. I noticed nothing, just slowly loping along, shoulders hunched, eyes to the ground.

I was awakened by something familiar. I saw Woolloomooloo Finger Wharf. Lang Walker, the billionaire whose house I bought at Woolooware Road, lived at the end of the wharf as did Ross, who lent me ten thousand dollars when I was in diabolical financial trouble. Across the road was the hotel where Jim, the Defence contract manager and myself sometimes had lunch. I turned my back on wealth and headed up the hill towards Kings Cross. I reached a small attractive park with plenty of grass on which homeless men were sitting and drinking. I started to cross the road. I lifted my head, my ears pricked up and I smelt danger. I was small and vulnerable. These people were rough and burly and I didn't feel safe. With my head down, eyes to the ground, the path funnelled me past a bus shelter towards an opening on the footpath leading to a low building with multiple angles and an awning. Poorly dressed men with their backs to the building sat on sleeping bags, reading. I instinctively felt safe as I sat down three metres away.

"You can't stay there, that's someone's spot," a voice said.

"Where can I sleep?"

"I don't know, try around the corner."

I moved around the building where there was a police station and a chemist. I sat on the footpath near two young men and a young woman.

"Someone's sleeping there," one of the young men said.

"Where can I sleep?"

"Dunno. Try Matthew Talbot," he said, pointing to a building across the road.

I immediately saw an old building surrounded by a high mesh fence with a cross on it. I walked along the fence and followed a small gap towards the start of the building, nosing around the side until I reached the entry door. I trotted up the ramp to the glass barricade. Entry to the inside of the hostel was impossible, the locked doors forbidding entry.

"Can I help you?" the huge man behind the glass asked. He was imposing but I didn't sense danger, only warmth.

"I'm looking for somewhere to sleep," I said.

"We're full, I'm sorry."

"Where can I go?"

"I don't know, I'm sorry, but you can always eat here. We will give you breakfast if you're here before eight o'clock. When the roller door shuts breakfast is finished."

I wandered back to the street where I sat near a thin man with a goatee beard.

"If you want to stay here you'll have to move to the other side of me," he said.

I sat beside him and we introduced ourselves, himself as BK, myself as Jimmy Black. We chatted about the book he was reading (which he had borrowed from the Matthew Talbot library), the politics of the day, and the Sydney City Council's attitudes to homelessness. I was relaxed and safe. After about half an hour we started to discuss my sleeping arrangements.

He said I should get cardboard out of the garbage bins as it was good insulation and I wouldn't get cold. I scavenged through the nearest garbage bins until I had enough cardboard to make a comfortable mattress. As I sat on my mattress I felt a connection with those around me. I was with my peers. It was the same feeling I had when I was with Brenda in Paris; the worries of the world melted away. As I became comfortable I started to function at a higher level. I told BK that I had to be at breakfast no later than eight a.m., I always slept in, and there was no way I would know what time it was.

"Don't worry about sleeping in, the cunts from the Council'll sweep you off the street real early. We're just fuckin garbage. They'll have your arse out of here well before eight o'clock. If you want to know the time get your lazy arse off the cardboard and check the parking meters, they'll tell you the time."

I was just starting to get cold when the men in uniform arrived, two of them.

"I hear you need blankets," one of the Salvos said.

"How do you know I need blankets?"

"Matthew Talbot rang and said someone on the street needed blankets. Plenty of people round here told us where you were."

With that he gave me a couple of blankets, grey cotton, so I knew I would be warm during the night. I settled in and noticed the footpath near the building gradually fill up as more and more people put their mattresses and sleeping bags on the ground and started to settle in for the night. There was a uniform: clothes were all grey and light brown, boots were scuffed and dilapidated, all hair was uncombed. Boots—that's what put me apart more than anything else. Mine were black RM Williams. As BK said, "Don't take them off or you'll spend the rest of the day barefoot." My clothes weren't worth stealing—jeans, T-shirt and a nondescript jumper. While not being a uniform they didn't stamp me as an outsider.

"I'm feeling a bit hungry," I remarked to BK.

"A food cart will be here in the next hour, there's plenty of food on the street."

He told me the food carts came most nights of the week, from various charities and church groups, but they were not super reliable. He advised me not to eat in Martin Place because it was too rough, and that there was a permanent food caravan at the end of Cathedral Street where I could always get food. I already knew I could get three meals a day from Matthew Talbot, but I just wanted to go there for breakfast. My instinct was to have breakfast at the same place each day, but not return for any other meal; it was a deeply ingrained habit.

I was just about to go to sleep when I remembered one more thing.

"What do I do with the blankets and cardboard during the day?" I asked BK.

BK was starting to doze off.

"Carry them with you all day you dumb cunt, or do what everyone else does—put them in the bins on the other street. The bins are locked during the day so cunts can't thieve our stuff. Anythin fuckin else before I go to sleep?"

"No."

I slept like a log. I had food, shelter, clothing and a friend. What more could I want? The next morning, I woke up and I was alone. I found the bins that BK had told me about and put my cardboard and blankets on top of everyone else's belongings. I meandered across to Matthew Talbot. Breakfast was in a huge room split into two. One half was packed with seats that faced a TV screen while the other half was filled with tables jammed together where over a hundred people could be fed at once. I noticed the dreaded roller door. I picked up a tray and joined the queue. It was a cafeteria, with porridge, boiled eggs, toast and coffee. It was good. I found a vacant spot and squeezed in. I was relaxed. No one talked to me, no one was friendly but the atmosphere was calm and I didn't feel threatened or alone. The air was filled with a faint smell of human odour. I didn't notice much, but I did notice that there wasn't any sartorial elegance. Nor was there arrogance or aggression. There were no smiles, no laughter, no real happiness, except that I was, if not happy, somewhat at peace. I noticed the blackboard advertised roast turkey and roast potato for lunch and meatballs and pasta for dinner.

The next day after breakfast I went downstairs for a communal shower. The shower floor had wooden slats, the place stunk of urine, but there was plenty of soap and the water was hot. I was homeless but determined not to look homeless. A friend of mine who owned a pig farm once told me that there were filthy pigs and clean pigs. I was determined to be a clean pig.

A couple of days later I bought a self-inflating mattress, a sleeping bag and rucksack, wire chain and lock from Paddy Pallin. I bought the most basic things I needed very cheaply, but they took a big chunk of my four hundred dollars. I also bought basic toiletries and a cheap T-shirt, underwear and socks so I had a change of clothes. I never paid for washing and drying. I was always able to piggy-back on to someone else's load at the laundromat. I shamelessly cadged on people. I didn't think of myself as wealthy, and given the way I was living and the rejection of everything I owned, I was, in my own mind, poor as a church mouse, and very content.

I quickly established a routine. Breakfast at Matthew Talbot, then the NSW State Library to read the *Sydney Morning Herald*. I hired a locker for a couple of dollars a day to store my haversack so I stopped using the homeless bin except for my cardboard. I had coffee at McDonalds in George Street after which I wandered around the city before an afternoon nap on a park bench in the Botanical Gardens near a pond. Late afternoons I returned home to my reserved spot on Cathedral Street, tied my locked haversack to a post and wandered about chatting to people. I didn't miss anyone. Not Josie, not the kids, not my friends. I never thought of anyone. I had all the social contact I needed and I was happy. My only decision was to choose which food cart I would eat from that night. I was a stray dog, loyal to the hand that fed me, sniffing around for secure shelter, moving away from danger, beholden to nobody, living from one experience to the next.

After five days on the street I ran out of my medication so I went to a local doctor's surgery recommended by BK. When I walked in the door, the surgery waiting room was full with about five people waiting. I approached the receptionist, a rotund middle-aged woman with reading glasses attached to a chain that hung around her neck. I was instinctively cautious; I didn't like people who needed a chain around their neck to keep tabs on their glasses.

"Can I help you?" she asked.

"I've run out of anti-depressants and I want to ask the doctor where I can get some."

"What's your name?"

"Jimmy Black, but that's not my real name."

"You will have to give me your real name. Everything here is confidential."

"No, it's not. If the police come here with a search warrant, how much confidentiality would I have then?"

I watched as her smile faded, lips tightened and eyes hardened. I knew straight away she was used to dealing with dross like me.

"Well, if you want the doctor to give you medication, you'll have to give me your real name otherwise I can't help you."

"I wasn't asking the doctor for medication, only where I could get anti-depressants. Anyhow I don't give a shit. I have no Aropax. In three days it'll be out of my system, and then there will be one less piece of garbage on the street, and the world will be a better place," I retorted as I turned to walk away.

"Please stay," she pleaded.

I ignored her and kept walking. As I was about to reach the door, a young man in his late teens or early twenties got out of his chair and partially blocked the exit. He motioned me to sit in his chair, which I meekly did as he patted me on the shoulder. A few minutes later the receptionist returned and put a pack of Arapax in my hand. As she did so she clasped her other hand in mine.

"Please take care of yourself," she said.

"You're an angel," I replied.

As I reached the door, the young man gripped my shoulder. For the first time, I felt I was a human being. That I was of value—not much, but at least some value. The touch, the words of human kindness meant the world to me.

I settled into my routine and started to actually think of the future. It was three weeks and the locker charges and cups of coffee each day at McDonalds were starting to drain what was left of my initial four hundred dollars. I was slowly becoming more aware of where I was and what I was doing to the point that I realised it wouldn't be long before I needed money. I didn't need much, but I needed to buy coffee and toiletries at the very least. I had to decide how I would get money. Begging like Brenda, or getting a part-time job were the only viable alternatives. I decided to ask BK, little knowing that he would make the decision for me.

I sat outside the chemist shop as BK approached. He noticed that the chemist had put a sandwich board on the footpath where we slept at night.

"What's that fuckin thing doing there?" he said.

"Don't worry BK. They shut in half an hour and it will be gone," I said, not comprehending that he was becoming agitated.

"The cunts should move it now." His eyes widened.

"It's not worth the hassle. Just leave it alone," I said.

He bent down, picked up the sandwich board and held it high above his head. I saw his eyes widen and go crazy and the sandwich board crashing towards my head. It smashed against the side of my head as I ducked. I lifted my head from the ground as he smashed the board onto my head again. I got up and staggered, dazed, into the chemist shop. I gave the assistant Josie's mobile so that she could pick me up.

Forty minutes later Josie arrived and stopped where I was standing in an isolated part of Cathedral Street. She had a wide smile on her face, but at the same time a look of concern. She was obviously happy to see me. I quickly jumped into the car as I didn't want anyone to see me in a car, let alone a Mercedes.

She was about to say something.

"I'm not coming home, I'm only here because I got bashed. I need to go to hospital," I said.

I was oblivious to Josie's tears and the distress on her face. We drove to Sutherland Hospital and Josie sat beside me very distressed while I sat engrossed in my own selfish world unaware of anything or anyone in my vicinity. Later, Josie took me from the hospital to home. I was still very sick, sore and sorry for myself.

I didn't know of the family meeting that had taken place after I disappeared. Josie, my children and my sisters knew that I had probably caught a train so was likely to be somewhere in the city. A list of fifteen places and agencies was compiled and a poster with my photo prepared and circulated. Josie, my children, siblings and friends physically searched the streets. Woolloomooloo police station was notified that I was a missing person. They were distraught with the worry of my disappearance and not knowing where I was or what I was doing. I had vanished.

After a few days on the street I had remembered that myself and Josie were supposed to be going to a farm at Neville with our closest friends to the Orange Forage, for which we had prepaid tickets. Our friends were sitting at the dining table discussing my disappearance, the air sombre, everyone sick with worry and the weekend totally ruined when my friend Greg's phone dinged with a message.

Safe and well, Jimmy Black was the message.

Greg immediately rang the phone.

"Can I speak to Russell? He just sent me a message," he told the person who answered the phone.

"Sorry. I was sitting in McDonalds in George Street when this old guy asked me if he could borrow my phone to send a message. He sent the message and disappeared."

All the places and agencies were revisited and my description now incorporating the name Jimmy Black was circulated. Josie needed and was given emotional support from all our family and friends. It was a sad and terrible time for everyone, except the perpetrator of the misery.

After I left hospital I returned home. Josie told everyone I wasn't normal and that I was withdrawn and strange. I saw family and friends but generally I was left alone. I gradually became a bit less withdrawn and started to move towards normality. At this point I didn't want to return to sleeping rough, possibly because I mostly disengaged from people around me, avoiding daily pressures while having my basic needs of food and shelter in a safe place met.

Soon after I returned home, I was surprised to receive a copy of the official transcript sent by the Sorbonne to Sydney University. The Sorbonne certified my results:

Subject	*Mark*	*Grade*
Philosophie et Histoire de sciences	13.5	C
Cours de Philosophie	12.25	C
Histoire de la logique et de la rhetorique	16	A
Enseingments optionnels	14.5	B
Options d'ouverture	14.5	B
Cours d'ouverture	14.5	B

These were the results I had expected. My lowest mark was 62.25% and highest mark 80%. I was mystified as to how the results were compiled and didn't recognise the names of some of the subjects. I didn't celebrate, I was too sick to care.

Two months after sleeping rough on the streets of Sydney Josie and I travelled to Europe with our friends. We planned to discover Rome, the Amalfi Coast, and relax on a Croatian cruise. I continued to take anti-depressants and my state of mind appeared to improve. It never occurred to me, or anyone else, that I was too sick to travel with a group of people, even friends. The holiday was a disaster. My behaviour was abominable; long rambling tirades, abusing waiters and continual threats of self-harm made my friends' lives miserable. On the Croatian cruise, a small boat with a couple of dozen people, ten minutes before one lunch I moved most of the tables, and reset each one, against the protestations of the crew, because I was unhappy with the seating arrangements. No one has invited me on an overseas trip since, and if I were me I wouldn't invite myself either. It was only in hindsight that I discovered I was totally unfit to travel as I had no ability to cope within a group. I lashed out at those around me to protect myself, to prevent people coming near me; it was antisocial, disruptive and unpleasant for those around me. Any connection I had to the Sorbonne and my life in Paris had been severed. I was too sick to comprehend how my stay in Paris had impacted my life.

I knew I needed treatment so, over the next nine months, I consulted a psychologist, a psychiatrist and spent time in hospital. Although my mental and emotional state gradually improved, this didn't stop me from seeking refuge on the streets. When my psychiatrist informed me I was "well enough" to be admitted back into hospital in two weeks, I felt compelled to sleep rough again that night. I was taking flight. I knew what hospital entailed and I intended to leave Sydney permanently.

The night two girls put blankets on me and tucked me in and said goodnight, I felt the warmth of their kindness and compassion. I lay on my cardboard, warm and cosy under the bright lights beneath the awning. I lay motionless, listening to the soft sounds of talking, the occasional traffic and footsteps of passersby. I was relaxed and happy. Thoughts started creeping into my head. I asked myself, what am I doing here? How did I get here? What sort of person am I? It was a confusing melange of questions and thoughts that rushed in and out of my mind. I became oblivious to my surroundings as I tried to answer some questions.

My thoughts were random, like peripatetic travellers going everywhere and anywhere, and never staying long in the same place. I travelled back to the Sorbonne and my oral exam. I had a choice of two topics, "Can we communicate our experience?" or "Are we what we experience?" I chose the first topic, but as I lay on the footpath I considered the second. Was I what I experienced, or was I something different? I concluded that my soul, my being was what I had experienced.

All experiences created us, mostly in ways that we were unaware. It was difficult to make a list of experiences from which I could determine which ones shaped my being, my values and who I was. I thought of the experiences that were the most important.

I lay still. I could now see stars—not very bright. The city lights always detracted from what would otherwise be a spectacular night sky display. I used to know the planets and constellations but I had forgotten, and I couldn't see most of them anyway.

I pictured the unpainted humpy at Hill End with its rickety verandah, where me and Uncle Role sat on old rocking chairs facing the dirt road that carried the occasional car to the nearby village. I relived pulling the old kettle off the fireplace, filling tea cups and sitting, drinking tea, yarning about whatever we wanted to yarn about, laughing and joking. My mind started walking the paddocks with the dogs, shooting rabbits, and watching the dogs penning sheep. My face became warm, my muscles relaxed as I lay on the street, mentally blacksmithing and timber clearing. I was swinging the blacksmith's hammer and the axe, working beside my uncle, with no demands, doing what I wanted to do at my own pace. Everything was done in its own time.

I felt a cramp in my side so I rolled on to my left side, as my mind moved to Berrara. I was in our boat with Bill anchoring across the current throwing out bread to burly for mullet.

Lying on my side, I experienced the expectation and thrill as I saw the mullet jumping in the distance and the pull on the line as I hooked the first fish. I was with Bill and we knew each other. We didn't have to say anything. We lived for what we did. All we needed was a fishing line, hooks and bread to be happy—the small boat was a bonus. If we didn't catch any fish it didn't matter, we just loved being together doing things.

My mind went blank. I had no vision, only a feeling. Of loss. I missed Brenda. I smiled as my mind saw the young woman who asked me for money in St. Germaine. I inwardly laughed as I heard her ask if I was interested in her mother. I joked to myself that at fifty-eight years of age her mother was too young for me. I thought about the hour a week, sometimes much more that we spent together, usually sitting at a café. I silently coughed as her cigarette smoke spiralled into my lungs. We sat drinking coffee, chatting about whatever my limited language skills allowed me to.

I rolled on my back and recalled what we talked about. I tried to think. I didn't offer her much about myself. I told her I had a wife, children and grandchildren but not much else. I reflected on what she gave me, letting me carry her child, how she talked about herself, her brother's problems, her sister and her boyfriend, where she lived and grew up. My feelings were confused. As I lay on my back I realised she had shared with me her most intimate feelings, her health issues, how much she earned on the streets. I saw the distress on her face when she thought her brother could go to jail, her joy when she saw her old home at Arad. I pictured her walking the street begging for money, I smiled as I remembered her purple boots with the holes in the soles, her shivering in the cold, without a coat, as she made sure I was safely on the bus. I relaxed when I was with her, I felt a connection. Maybe there was, maybe there wasn't, but I left the pressures of study and my self-imposed expectations at the door of Damien's apartment when I went to see her.

When I was with Brenda, I was with my Uncle Role and Bill. That's spiritually where I needed to be. I was meant to live life, here, now, simply, not making money, doing commercial deals or trying to show others how clever I was. I had to live just as I was now, lying under the stars, conscious of everything around me, with nothing, yet happy. I knew I wasn't meant to be sleeping rough. I needed to be surrounded by those that loved me. I shifted restlessly. The night had suddenly become strangely silent. There was no traffic, no people nearby, just a light hum of city life.

I knew where my soul was, but what sort of person was I? I thought about the twenty-five euros and packets of cigarettes I gave Brenda each time we met. I restlessly moved on the cardboard as I envisaged my routine of emptying my pockets of credit cards and money when I met her so that she couldn't wheedle money out of me. I had a wry smile when I rationalised that I did it to protect myself.

I pictured the expensive meal I shouted Damien and the first-class flight back to Australia. I thought about my agreement with Brenda that I would pay her twenty euros for French conversation. When we last met I didn't give her twenty euros because I didn't think I needed to. I reflected that Brenda was poor, a gypsy, a woman, a social outcast, and had very few choices in life, yet she had emotionally shared her life with me. I became upset when I pictured her purple boots with the holes in the soles. She wanted new boots, and I said no. I thought about the two young women who put blankets on me, the people at Matthew Talbot Hostel, the Punchbowl church group. I realised that I was a powerful, privileged, rich, white man, and a heartless, self-entitled arsehole. That was not who I wanted to be. I wanted to be the person who would unthinkingly buy Brenda new boots, buy her a coat, listen to her with compassion and understanding, not use her to improve my French. I lay on the ground, forlorn and sad. I missed her.

Thirty-one

A couple of months after the holiday to Europe I told the psychologist I intended to admit myself to residential rehabilitation. He strongly advised against it on the basis that I was improving anyway, and going to hospital wouldn't solve anything. I didn't believe him. I knew I wouldn't leave hospital recovered, but I expected my recovery to be supercharged. I made the choice.

Enrolling at South Pacific Private Hospital (SPPH) was as difficult as enrolling at the Sorbonne. It is not everyone who graduates from normal to so sick that you can have free board and lodging (I was a member of HCF) at a private facility, near the beach at Collaroy.

I filled out the questionnaire, passed the phone interview, and was then interviewed by the hospital psychiatrist. I passed all tests with flying colours—the hospital determined I was severely depressed.

I arrived at the hospital on the appointed day of admission. In the foyer of what looked like a big old house in need of tender love and care, I waited. The most striking feature was the sign 'Miracles do happen'. After more interviews, more forms, more questions, I was ready to roll. Bill escorted me to a room where I put my bag on the bed. Bill was a big man in early fifties with a weather-beaten face, and a demeanour that wouldn't be out of place in a prison watchhouse.

"Tip your belongings on the bed," he demanded.

"Why?"

"I'm going to check for contraband."

"There isn't any."

"Do what I tell you."

I dutifully tipped the contents of my bag on to the bed and shock, horror, Bill confiscated the contraband I was sneaking into the hospital. The *Sydney Morning Herald*, a self-improvement book and my asthma medication were all forbidden. He confiscated my mobile phone. Bill meticulously noted each item and I signed a document to ensure they would be returned on my release.

"Is there anything you want?" he asked, in an unexpected tone of kindness.

"If I gave you a glass of water, could you bring back a glass of wine?"

With a loud snort, he turned on his heel. I took it as a no.

The rules Bill laid out were pretty simple. No television (except for half an hour a night), no reading material not supplied by the hospital, no phone calls (except once a week for a few minutes), visitors allowed only on Sunday afternoon, and no one was allowed to leave the hospital grounds except under the supervision of staff. All meals were supplied and caffeine was a prohibited substance.

The heart of treatment at SPPH was the group sessions. These were small groups of patients led by a trained psychologist. I enjoyed my first group session. We all stood in a circle and held hands; I hadn't held hands in a circle since I played 'Ring a ring a rosie' in kindergarten. We said a prayer-like thing that entreated us to deal with the things we could control and accept the things we couldn't control.

One of my favourite pastimes at the hospital was the daily walk to the beach. We all stood at the entrance to the hospital under the watchful eyes of two staff members, wearing our nametags, and walked en masse to the beach. Surfing or swimming was forbidden 'for insurance reasons'. I really enjoyed being publicly paraded as an inmate of a rehab hospital.

I didn't settle in to the hospital. I didn't cope and was very destructive. I was aggressive and antagonistic to staff and patients who came near me. It was my natural defence mechanism.

I was dozing off while a young counsellor was delivering a lecture on recovering from addiction when my ears pricked up.

"You can only beat addiction with the help of a higher power, you cannot do it yourself." That was consistent with the serenity prayer we chanted in each group session "to the God and Goddess of our understanding".

"You don't have to believe in a particular God, and relying on the Church is not the way. You have to find your own God, your own higher power," she intoned. Having spent a semester at the Sorbonne studying philosophy, I couldn't help myself.

"That's rubbish, churches exist to bring God to their congregation. The Church helps you find God, that's the whole point of prayer. Relying on the Church is an ideal way to find God," I loudly interjected.

"Look at how priests molest young boys. The Church is a problem not the answer," a patient called out.

"Don't confuse the religion with the institutional church. There is no problem with the religion itself, and believing in a Christian God is as effective as believing in any higher power," I replied.

"How can you believe in God, when all the Church does is protect itself," someone else said.

"Don't generalise. I don't like the Catholic Church, but when I went to live on the street it was the Matthew Talbot Hostel, a Catholic institution, that gave me food and showers and gave me love, respect and compassion. We have to recognise the good that Catholics do."

A debate about complex issues involving the Church, faith and the practice of religion ensued. It destroyed the lecture. I was oblivious to the fact that my intervention didn't help other patients.

I lasted eight days. I was very frightened, and totally unable to cope in the hospital environment. I couldn't sleep in the room with other people, so I slept in the common room and refused to budge. I physically fought the nursing staff who tried to remove me. Despite my problems, the hospital staff did everything they could to persuade me to stay, but staying at the hospital was voluntary so they couldn't keep me in. I didn't want to go home, so I went to my safe haven, a spare cottage I owned next to my caravan park. A week later I realised my mistake; without some radical treatment, I would never get better.

I applied to be readmitted and was refused. Steve Sutton, who ran the hospital day to day, said I was too sick to be in hospital, but would allow me to return if a psychiatrist certified me well enough to be treated in hospital. I immediately sought psychiatric help, and for the next six months consulted a psychiatrist twice a week.

The psychiatrist, Brian Gascoyne, said he would give me medication for depression but preferred that I deal with the depression with meditation. I was familiar with meditation and followed his advice. Meditation alters the brain, and my depression was ultimately defeated solely with meditation. Meditation, with cognitive behaviour therapy, also helped me overcome the underlying psychological problems.

It took six months of two psychiatrist sessions a week before I was well enough to be admitted, once again, to SPPH. The first week back at SPPH was difficult. I found it difficult to cope, and was very aggressive towards staff and patients. I refused to participate in some activities, blatantly disobeyed rules, and was put on a contract.

The hospital had a system; if a patient transgressed the rules, they were counselled, and put on a contract to help with their recovery. The hospital asserted that the contract was a form of support. I went swimming on the daily walk, a breach of the hospital rules, and was put on a contract that forbade me to leave the hospital at all. It was a form of punishment. Each morning all the patients gathered together. Each patient, in turn, had to state their problem (co-dependency, drug addiction and alcoholism were favourites), and whether they were on a contract. On the surface it would be easy to see the public revelation of a contract as public humiliation, however in the caring environment of the hospital it didn't seem like that.

I enjoyed the pre-bedtime activities. After we ate and before lights out, we were allowed to sit in the common room but not allowed to talk. One of the patients, Anna, was a young girl, about twenty years old, with a morphine addiction. She had a beautiful singing voice and continually sang, mainly to herself. One night we were sitting round the table, undertaking our intellectual nourishment—colouring in. I liked the colouring in. I hadn't practised it since kindergarten, and I was a bit ashamed it wasn't up to the standard of my preschool grandchildren.

Anna started to softly sing. "Ssssh," whispered another patient, "You're not allowed to talk."

"She's not talking, she's singing," I whispered.

"Let her sing," others whispered.

And so she sang, for an hour. I was lost in my world, colouring in, listening to a beautiful voice. I was at peace with the world. I was sad when she was discharged a week later.

I was in the blue group for group sessions. It consisted of a variety of people from different walks of life. A senior banker, French housewife, unemployed ice addict, French advertising executive, solicitor from an international law firm and others. We had an inexperienced therapist, Jenny, straight out of Sydney University with a first class honours degree in psychology. Young, enthusiastic and caring, she somehow unified us all, despite our different ages, problems and socio-economic circumstances. With our innermost secrets revealed and discussed, in a non-judgemental, trusting environment, together with the general care within the hospital, I started to improve.

All group sessions within the hospital were conducted according to a formula. They started with a confidentiality pledge. We sat in a circle and in turn said who we were, why were in hospital and how we felt. I did pretty well at this. I knew my name, and why I was in hospital. How I felt was a bit problematic. Helpful as ever, the hospital had a sign pinned to the wall that set out the range of allowable feelings.

"My name is Russell, I suffer from depression, co-dependency [everyone acquired this affliction in hospital. It was like measles—very hard to avoid once the infection spread], and I feel—[pause to provide a sense of authenticity]—joy and guilt."

The session ended with a reading from a book which had some obscure relevance to the session. We stood in a circle, holding hands while reciting the serenity prayer. We finished by throwing our hands in the air and yelling "Go Blue."

By the end of the first week I had settled quite comfortably into the group sessions.

"Would anyone tell me if I am saying things wrong or doing things I shouldn't be doing?" I asked.

"No, I'm too afraid you'll attack me," the French woman said.

"She's right Russell, you've got a really nasty streak. Everyone's scared of you," the banker added.

The room was silent. I had a capacity to process information almost instantaneously. I thought of how for decades I had spoken to Josie. I had an acerbic tongue, a sarcastic, vicious sense of humour, and I sometimes made jokes at Josie's expense. Very amusing to everyone except Josie. I thought of how I treated Brenda. Unlike Josie, I never verbally abused Brenda. To the contrary, however I did exploit her for my own benefit. I clearly saw who I was, and I didn't like me.

"I will change," I said.

Two weeks earlier I had lain on cardboard in Cathedral Street and discovered who I was, and that I wanted to be someone different. The French woman and the banker's words provided the catalyst for me to take the action I needed to change. I made a conscious decision to totally alter my behaviour, not just within the hospital but how I lived my life from then on. I would never be Mother Teresa, but the words I heard changed my life. I changed because within my being was a passion for change that was generated solely within myself. I knew I had to change, I wanted to change, however, for any change to occur there had to be a point at which action commenced. The words forced me to act. To ignore what was said would have negated everything I had decided I wanted to be when I lay in Cathedral Street thinking about Brenda.

Twice a day, during group and other sessions, I had to publicly reveal my feelings. I no longer had to look at a list to work out how I felt. The knot in my stomach and tightening of my chest screamed Shame and Guilt. Love and Joy disappeared. The next week, I left the group to do 'Changes'.

Not everyone was allowed to do Changes. I was one of the chosen few. Why, I didn't know. Changes meant spending five days, all day, in the same group of ten patients, plucked seemingly at random from the prison—oops—hospital population. It replaced the lectures, activities and normal group activities. Each person in the group shared their innermost secrets, things never discussed in group sessions or with other patients. It was extremely distressing. How on earth could an uncle take his niece to hospital to see his newborn baby, and rape her in the car on the way home? Why does a father have regular sex with his twelve-year-old daughter, and her mother, knowing about it, do nothing? The distress, hurt and irreparable damage inflicted upon these women caused me to rethink my own situation. Each person had to recount their stories in graphic details. I was the last cab off the rank.

What could I say? I grew up in a home devoid of physical abuse. I never experienced sexual abuse, my mother never worked, my father had his issues, but compared to what I had just heard, he was a saint. I had a good education, I was encouraged, in fact made, to stay at school and go to university. I had wonderful holidays at Berrara and Hill End. Both my parents loved me—sure they made mistakes, but they did the best they could for all their children. I heard nine harrowing stories of the worst type of abuse. I had to think of something. Most importantly it had to be true.

I recounted a sexual encounter I had as a ten-year-old which technically constituted abuse, but in reality was something I enjoyed. It was absolutely pathetic and I knew it. I was embarrassed to pretend it was abuse but it was the best I could do.

The week after Changes I rejoined my blue group and resumed normal activities. I had dramatically changed. I was happy, settled, enthusiastic about my treatment, starting to integrate socially with the other patients and co-operate with the nursing staff and counsellors. I knew I was really sick; that's why I was in hospital, but why, when my issues were so insignificant compared to others?

In some ways, I changed in a way that undermined the hospital treatment process.

Each day when the patients met, part of the process was to deal with the expression of feelings.

"Russell, can I share with you please?"

"Yes, Rachel."

"When we were standing in line at breakfast I said hello to you and you ignored me. I felt rejected, and it reminded me of the times my father didn't take any notice of me."

How could I acknowledge you in a queue when you speak in a voice so soft it is harder to hear than a dog whistle, I thought to myself.

"I hear you, Rachel." I said.

The concept was not to discuss the merits of what was behind the feelings; the basis of the feelings might be wrong, but the feelings themselves were always real. All that was required was for me to acknowledge that I knew how she felt. Later that day I spoke to Rachel and apologised, explaining that I didn't hear her.

I did something a little different.

"Betty can I share with you?"

"Yes, Russell," Betty hesitatingly said, not knowing what was coming next.

"When I hear you playing the piano, I feel very happy. It reminds me of the times I sat in the bath as my daughters played the piano. It made me feel nostalgic and happy."

"Thank you, Russell," was the surprised response.

Soon everyone jumped onto the feel-good bandwagon, which was not the point of the exercise. Teaching people to express difficult negative feelings was the object.

As I improved, the hospital gave me some responsibilities. I ran the morning yoga class—I arose early, cleared the chairs in the room, and switched on the projector. I also conducted the evening meditation class—I switched on the CD player.

I had difficulty with the model on which my treatment was based. Having spent a semester studying philosophy at the Sorbonne, I could never accept, without question, what was being pushed down my throat. The fundamental tenant of treatment was that addiction, depression or other mental issues arose from childhood trauma. This trauma led to adaptive behaviour, called 'acting out' that was 'more than' or 'less than' normal. In my group, we each recounted the trauma we suffered as a child. It was an integral part of the treatment, everything flowed from this premise. I struggled to find trauma in my childhood. I wished someone had belted me, abused me, abandoned or neglected me. I would then have an excuse for my illness. Mother is the nature of invention, so I found the trauma.

For the first eighteen months of my life, I was doted on, adored, totally attached to my mother. When Greg was born, I was abandoned. Six children were born in nine years and my mother had no time for me. My great grandmother lived nearby, and came every day to our house to look after me. She was kind, nurturing, doted on me and I loved her. Every psychological problem I ever had I was now able to sheet home to my mother—I was abandoned, the attachment to my mother broken—I suffered damage that led to my adaptive behaviour. I embraced the concept, but it was totally untrue. If I had any problems at all, they more likely came from the patriarchal family created by my father.

Hume and Kant distinguished emotion from reason. Intellectually, I believed the model was flawed. Emotion, however, didn't think. It was instinctive, undirected and uncontrolled. The improvement in my emotional state was dramatic. The tools I was given to live my life were critical in my future recovery. I still needed years of regular psychiatric sessions and months of out-patient stints in SPPPH. The hospital mantra was to trust the process. I trusted the process and eventually recovered. The French had a saying— It worked in practice, but did it work in theory? Who cares if it didn't work in theory, if it worked.

Epilogue

After I left hospital, I continued to consult Dr. Gascoyne twice a week. There was a set routine. I would sit on a couch, he would sit on a chair, facing me.

"Tell me what comes up," he would say.

I would then talk about the first thing that came into my head. I talked about many things, my conflicts, worries, fears, goals, always specifically. Brian never told me anything. He just kept asking questions and let me meander through the answers. The questions always led to an outcome, one I reached of my own accord. I was aware of my dialectic teaching technique, and techniques I used as a lawyer to cross-examine witnesses, so that they answered a crucial question in a way that suited my purpose. I found this different process intriguing, and from time to time answered Brian's questions in a way that I figured would lead to a further question, another answer, another question, and so on, until I reached the conclusion I had thought of when he asked the first question. In my delusional state, I thought I was clever. I was, but I doubt I ever fooled Brian.

About six months after I left hospital, I met with Brian. I was not relaxed, in fact I was quite testy.

"What's the point of what we are doing?" I asked.

"You need to grow."

"What do you mean, I need to grow? That's meaningless bullshit. What's your diagnosis?"

He looked at me, sat up in his chair, and looked me in the eye.

"You have the emotional intelligence of a fourteen-year-old. We have to develop your emotional intelligence."

"OK, I get that, but how are these fireside chats achieving anything? What's the process?"

"I don't know." He paused. "I can't tell you how it works, but I can tell you it works."

"How long will it take before I reach emotional adulthood?"

"As long as it takes."

As I later reflected on what Brian said, I understood the consequences. I was a nightmare of a husband but related well to my children and their friends. I thought, *Poor Josie, fancy being married to a teenage boy*. On the other hand, I dealt with my children in a non-judgemental way. I often spent time helping our friends' kids, I emotionally related to them, and had wisdom, knowledge and experience that was valuable.

Understanding that I lacked emotional intelligence gave me a framework to understand what had happened to me. I had studied the concept of experience at the Sorbonne, both in Philosophy Modern, Philosophy and History of Science and General Philosophy. It was a very important element of philosophy. The study of experience encompasses the role of reason and emotion. Kant believed the basis of morality was reason, Hume that it was emotion. Hume also believed that the sole source of knowledge was experience. Hume in his explanation for the workings of the mind started with perceptions, which he divided into impressions of sensation (original impressions) and impressions of reflection (secondary reflections). If I was hit by a car, when I remembered the accident I was remembering an idea. This memory led to the secondary reflection of fear that caused me to take protection against future accidents. It was the sensation created from the memory that motivated my behaviour. So the drivers of my behaviour was how I felt about previous experience, processed by my child-like emotional intelligence.

When I started to struggle at the Sorbonne, I made decisions from the viewpoint of a teenager—I could only relate to childhood experience. The things I enjoyed most in my youth were my holidays at Berrara, fishing, prawning with hand-held nets and pressure lamps at night in nearby Swan Lake, no shirt or shoes, no trappings of wealth, the need for nothing, and living in Hill End with my uncle Role, in a dump. I loved it. I emotionally travelled to where I was happy and secure; Berrara and Hill End. In Paris, it was Brenda. She showed me the streets of Paris and I understood it was possible to survive, to live, to dream—without a jacket, holes in boots, existing only on wits. I was happy and calm when we were together. I didn't realise it, but it was a reflection of my experience. When I thought of her, after we finally said good-bye, the thought was a reflection, the emotions were only positive.

When, on my return to Sydney, my coping mechanism collapsed, I acted emotionally. Normally when people acted emotionally, such action was tempered by reason. Considering consequences was not emotional, but a function of reason. A feature of mental illness was the absence of reason. When, for no apparent reason, I left my home, I hadn't any capacity for reason, so my action was dictated by my most primitive and basic emotions. I went to the only place I knew that was safe, a place I expected from experience to make me happy, the streets of Sydney, not far, emotionally, from Brenda and the streets of Paris.

My treatment at South Pacific Private Hospital taught me how to deal with my emotions and to feel and understand them. The treatment had an underlying model that, in my opinion, lacked intellectual credibility, but worked, because in the process it increased my emotional intelligence. As my emotional intelligence improved I made decisions differently, as an adult not a child.

Over time I learnt to express my emotions, didn't take things personally, stopped being solely goal-orientated. It took a long time, but I meditated, noticed things around me, stayed present, while still setting goals but they were not the be all and end all, and I started to enjoy the journey. My attitudes to people around me changed, old habits of denigration disappeared and I became more pleasant to be around. I was calmer, more content. I was not perfect by any means but as I got older I was, as Brian said, 'growing' all the time. I became more self-aware, or more accurately more aware of the impact and damage my actions caused those around me, particularly Josie.

In the early 1980s I frequented the Manor House restaurant in Balmain. It was a very old heritage house set in a magnificent garden. The food was a hatted standard and the wine cellar extensive. It was very expensive. I knew the owner Rob Manning, a rounded, middle-aged man of impeccable taste, with a charming and accommodating persona. Rob agreed that Josie and I could be married at the Manor House, under the huge gum tree surrounded by shrubs, with lights dangling from the boughs. A special and romantic setting. I knew it would be wonderful. Our reception was a dinner in a quiet corner of the restaurant. We only had six guests; our parents, a brother and sister and my two children.

"Are we ready to go Rob?" I said when we all arrived on our wedding night.

"Ready for what, Russell?" Rob said.

He forgot we were going to be married. The only space available was the cloakroom, which is where we were married. The cloakroom was shambolic and had to be cleared so we could squeeze in. I was annoyed, upset and disappointed, emotions which were overwhelmed and crushed with the joy and anticipation of our imminent marriage. The reception was a round table plonked smack bang in the middle of the restaurant. When Josie married me for better or worse, worse had a head start.

I couldn't really imagine what Josie had endured, emotionally. Time is never turned back, and I knew, as I got better, the hurt I had inflicted on Josie, my children and friends. I couldn't undo it, but I was, and am, sorry. I always knew I had redeeming features, it was just hard to identify and find them. At times I lost everything material, yet despite my best efforts I never lost the crucial things of life—the family and friends around me, even though I deserved to, for which I am forever grateful.

When I went to the Sorbonne I knew I was the oldest student, and yet, I didn't know I was also the youngest. I don't know how old I am emotionally, but I'm no longer a teenage boy.

Acknowledgements

This book, cathartic in nature, could only be written with the support and indulgence of family and friends. My wife Josie read and commented on all the important aspects of my life during our time together. My friends: Greg and Mandy; Sue and Kieran; Jenny and Jeff; John and Marica; and the Mullane boys Josh, Jack, Tyson and Angus; contributed throughout my writing journey. My sister Bronwyn and Ric Cilona provided encouragement and gave me cogent advice. Finally, my Wednesday writing group helped me hone my writing skills, such as they are, with constructive comments and encouragement.

    I am grateful for the professional help I received. Sarah Klenbolt my teacher at the Sydney Community College and mentor of the writing class has been instrumental in guiding me to finish this book. Alicia Walsh, my editor, tore the original draft apart and helped me restructure the story to make it the best that it could be. Without Alicia, this would be a very different book. I am appreciative of Thomasin Litchfield's copy editing.

www.ingramcontent.com/pod-product-compliance
Ingram Content Group UK Ltd.
Pitfield, Milton Keynes, MK11 3LW, UK
UKHW021323180426
11947UKWH00017B/1396